300/105

CLINICAL
TRAINING for
PASTORAL
CARE

CLINICAL
TRAINING for
PASTORAL
CARE

by
DAVID BELGUM

THE WESTMINSTER PRESS
Philadelphia

COPYRIGHT, MCMLVI, BY W. L. JENKINS

Scripture references, taken from the *Revised Standard Version of the Bible* unless otherwise noted, are copyrighted 1946 and 1952 by the Division of Christian Education of the National Council of Churches, and are used by permission.

Library of Congress Catalog Card Number: 56–5102

PRINTED IN THE UNITED STATES OF AMERICA

CONTENTS

Preface   5

1. Pastoral Concern for the Sick   9

2. The Health Team   21

3. Resources of the Pastor   47

4. The Pastoral Call   68

5. Learning from Clinical Experience   77

Conclusion:
    The Larger Perspective   128

Suggested Readings   135

PREFACE

THIS book is offered as a guide to students of pastoral care, whether they are in theological schools and clinical training centers or actively engaged in the parish ministry. Since such training is often given in the hospital setting, it seemed necessary to provide some orientation to the nature of the hospital and of the functions performed within it, the relationship of the church to the hospital as a social institution, and a method by which pastoral care can be learned while practiced in the laboratory of human suffering.

Parish pastors, who are traditionally called upon to visit the sick, need an opportunity to re-examine this aspect of their ministry with a fresh, critical analysis. Ministerial associations may use this book as a guide for a series of discussions led by some competent supervisor well versed in the theory of interpersonal relations and the techniques of counseling. Many pastors have found it helpful to write up some of their pastoral calls in detail (using a form similar to that recommended in Chapter 5) as a corrective check against the development of ineffective methods, habits, and mannerisms. It is hoped that many pastors will be stimulated by these chapters to rethink critically their approach to pastoral calling, ministry to the sick, and pastoral counseling; and that it can serve as a guide to self-criticism and professional as well as personal growth.

Hospital chaplains also need to evaluate their work from time to time in order to grow professionally. They need to rethink their interprofessional relationships, their approach to patients, and their use of pastoral resources.

Perhaps some alert reader will go a step farther and initiate some practical research in this fascinating field of the Christian ministry.

Surely our professional responsibility calls for as keen observation, as accurate recording, and as honest thinking as that required by our friends in the physical and social sciences.

Finally, this book is offered with a prayer that those who read it might be stimulated and challenged to minister with increasing effectiveness and devotion in their high calling of providing pastoral care for the sick.

CLINICAL
TRAINING for
PASTORAL
CARE

◁ 1 ▷

PASTORAL CONCERN FOR THE SICK

THE men in white coats gathering around a conference table at University Hospital were not doctors. They were clergymen from a half dozen states and Canada: an Anglican priest, a Baptist Army chaplain, Congregational, Lutheran, and Methodist pastors, ministers from the United Church of Canada, and an assortment of theological students. They were brought together by an intense desire to improve their understanding and practice of pastoral care. Interestingly and appropriately, their pastoral concern for the sick had led them to seek this training in a hospital setting where the need for pastoral care is urgent though not always obvious.

Parish ministers are keenly aware of the wide range of personal problems and disrupted social relations that cry out for adequate help from their congregations. There is a corresponding growing awareness of a need for better and fuller preparation to meet these challenges competently. It is not unusual to find within the average congregation people on the verge of mental illness and others in state hospitals, families rent asunder by divorce, eager businessmen whose bodies are breaking down under the stress of prolonged and accelerating competition, the unwanted and neglected child, as well as the unwanted and lonely aged. In the face of all this, no wonder pastors are seeking guidance.

WHY CLINICAL PASTORAL EDUCATION

Many a theological student looks forward to his first pastoral call on a hospitalized parishioner with dread and insecurity. Pastors look back upon their first ministry to the dying or in premarital counseling and wonder how they managed to stumble through in spite of themselves. It is a big step to pass from being a sheltered student to assuming the full responsibility of a minister of the gospel, supposedly prepared to meet all the great issues of life.

In order to bridge this gap, an intermediate stage has been found helpful. Seminary students can experience partially what it is like to be a pastor by performing limited pastoral functions under careful supervision. One of the most profitable of these functions, from an educational point of view, is calling on the sick.

Clinical pastoral training is becoming assimilated into the theological curriculum as an integral part of practical theology. Thus theory and practice can go hand in hand. However, such training is also of great benefit to men who have finished the seminary course. In fact, it becomes clear to a clergyman of some years' experience that there are many people in his parish whom he could serve far more effectively if he had a deeper insight into the dynamics of personality and interpersonal relationships as well as techniques and methods of using his pastoral resources. Therefore, practically every clinical training program has some pastors of experience enrolled.

Such role training has been found useful in other professions where the rigidity that comes from insecurity and fear of the new, unfamiliar task can be minimized by gradual initiation into the new role. This is true of the medical internship, supervised field work for social workers, or the student nurses' training program. Clinical training is a form of positive emotional education (sometimes emotional re-education), which establishes wholesome attitudes and behavior patterns appropriate to the respective role.

Medical students had benefited from supervised practical work with people for a long time before the full implications of this method were seen for theological education and the ministry. Roughly thirty years have elapsed since such pioneers as Dr. William S. Keller, of Cincinnati; Chaplain Anton T. Boisen, at Worcester State Hospital; and Dr. Richard C. Cabot, of Boston, took the initial steps in providing clinical training for seminarians and pastors. At present, a large number of training centers are conducted under the auspices of theological schools, in connection with councils of churches, and under the Council for Clinical Training, Inc., and the Institute of Pastoral Care, Inc. The following four goals for this training are agreed upon by the latter two organizations:

1. To enable the student to gain a fuller understanding of people, their deeper motivations and difficulties, their emotional and spiritual strengths and weaknesses.

2. To help the student discover more effective methods of ministering to individuals and groups, and to intensify his awareness of the unique resources, responsibilities, and limitations of the clergy.

3. To help the student learn to work more co-operatively with representatives of other professions and to utilize community resources which may lead toward more effective living.

4. To further the knowledge of problems met in pastoral care by providing opportunities for relevant and promising research. (See article compiled by the Department of Pastoral Services of the National Council of the Churches of Christ in the U.S.A., "Opportunities for Study, Training, and Experience in Pastoral Psychology — 1955," *Pastoral Psychology,* Vol. 5, No. 50, January, 1955, pp. 22–40.)

It is interesting to compare the above formally stated goals with those of a group of students. One such group of pastors and students, with whom the author worked as instructor, hoped to achieve the following goals during their period of study:

1. To learn to steer a middle course between the dangers of "professionalism" and "sentimentality," or between "objectivity" and "subjectivity."

2. To avoid winning persons to the pastor rather than to Christ.

3. To learn to keep from talking too much.

4. To improve my own personal habits and appearance, discipline and administration.

5. To learn how to be a brother to people, to get along with people in groups, to give and take criticism graciously.

6. To learn to be able to accept people as they are.

7. To learn to recognize danger signals in life situations.

8. To avoid rationalization of personal problems by posing them as theological or intellectual problems. (From the syllabus compiled and used by Chaplain Malcolm B. Ballinger at the Summer School of Pastoral Care at the University of Michigan, Ann Arbor, Michigan, summer, 1951.)

Note how practical the students' own goals are and how many of them involve their own personality growth in the sense of emotional role training. At the end of the summer course, all eight students agreed that their own objectives had been advanced and some indicated real appreciation for their progress.

Thus clinical pastoral training arose to meet a specific need in theological education, to bridge the gap between theory and practice. Although this is a recent movement or emphasis, the role of pastor of the sick is ancient indeed; and it is necessary to view this trend in its historical perspective, dating back to the ancient concern of religion for illness and the restoration of health.

An Ancient Tradition

Modern pastors follow in a path marked out by religion's traditional concern for sickness and healing. Primitive societies, as well as the cultured Greeks, considered priest and medicine man synonymous. Healing was one of the priestly functions in Greek temples.

Although the Hebrews were a nomadic people, and therefore not inclined, as were the Greeks, to establish permanent temples in the early part of their history, there was a moral attitude toward the sick and the stranger which can be considered an antecedent to the institutional care of the sick in hospitals. The Jews were anxious to provide for the needy, such as the stranger, the fatherless, and the widow. Often the sick were provided for by segregation; lepers were classified as " unclean " and lived in the hills. It was left for later times to integrate the idea of hospitality and segregation with the needs of the sick and combine the two elements into the hospital as an institution.

The healing miracles of Jesus indicate a change of attitude toward sickness. Instead of merely protecting the community by segregating the sick, the unfortunate victim was to be ministered to, healed, and cared for. The parable of the Good Samaritan portrays the wounded man treated with utmost consideration, brought to an inn, and cared for until he recovered. When Jesus healed lepers, he sent them to the priests to have their healing certified. The Great Physician instituted healing as a regular part of the work of the disciples: " They will lay their hands on the sick, and they will recover" (Mark 16:18, Margin). When our Lord sent out the Seventy, he instructed them to "heal the sick in it and say to them, 'The kingdom of God has come near to you'" (Luke 10:9).

Peter's reputation for healing became so great "that they brought forth the sick into the streets, and laid them on beds and couches, that at the least the shadow of Peter passing by might overshadow some of them" (Acts 5:15). A method of caring for the sick, described in James 5:14, 15, finally grew into the sacrament of extreme unction. "Is any sick among you? let him call for the elders of the church; and let them pray over him, anointing him with oil in the name of the Lord; and the prayer of faith shall save the sick, and the Lord shall raise him up; and if he have committed sins, they shall be forgiven him."

As the Church became more complexly organized, care of the sick was also institutionalized. It took a special crisis to bring the needs of the sick into the open. "Naturally it was travelers attacked by illness that called for the greatest pity and anxiety. This was the origin of hospitals . . . , the first of which was founded in the last quarter of the fourth century, A.D., on account of a famine which had caused a deadly epidemic" (G. Bonet-Maury, "Hospitality (Christian)," in James Hastings, ed., *Encyclopedia of Religion and Ethics,* VI, p. 804).

Chrysostom established seven different hospitals about A.D. 400, which would be considered by modern Church welfare agencies to be quite comprehensive in their coverage of human needs. There was an inn for strangers and travelers, a hospital for the treatment of acute illness, another hospital for chronic patients, a home for orphans and a home for the aged, a home for the reception of the poor, and another for all kinds of destitutes.

During the Middle Ages numerous monastic orders and lay brotherhoods cared for the sick. To meet the health crises of the great crusades, a series of migrant wars leaving wounded along the way and spreading disease, military monastic orders were established. The Knights of St. John of Jerusalem and others established many hospitals along the route from northern Europe to the Holy Land and ministered to the sick along the way. John of Avila pioneered a work among the sick that became famous as the Hospitalers.

Sometimes a hospital would be founded by an order, and in other cases a religious order would be born from an unusually successful hospital program, so that branch hospitals would be sponsored by the mother institution.

It is illuminating to notice that the spiritual care of patients in the Hôtel Dieu (a thirteenth century hospital in Paris) was quite complete and elaborate. Everything possible was done to maintain the patient's spiritual life.

> On entering the hospital, the patient, if a Christian, went to confession and received Holy Communion, in order that peace of mind might benefit bodily health. . . . According to their ability, the sick performed the duties of prayer, attendance at Mass, and reception of the sacraments. They were especially recommended to pray for their benefactors, for the authorities, and for all who might be in distress. At nightfall a sort of litany was recited in the wards, each verse of which began: " *Seignors malades, proies por,*" etc. They were often cheered by the visits of persons of high station or of noble rank and charitable disposition, like Catherine of Sweden; Margaret, Queen of Scotland, Margaret, Duchess of Lorraine; King Louis IX of France (James J. Walsh, " Religion and Health," in *Catholic Encyclopedia,* Charles G. Herbermann, *et al.,* eds., 1910, VII, p. 486).

These brief references to the role of the church in the care of the sick should make it clear that such concern is not new or unique with our generation. Rather, let us look upon the current interest in pastoral care as a renewal of interest and concern.

RECENT TRENDS

Since the beginning of the present century, the modern hospital has really come into its own with increasing knowledge of bacteriology, aseptic surgery, and scientific chemotherapy. Hospitals vary from great teaching and research centers to custodial institutions. They are built, and their policies established, by wealthy benefactors, Church bodies, fraternal organizations, and the Government (on city, county, state, and Federal levels). To consider the modern hospital is to approach a complex social phenomenon.

Although the Church has a long history of pastoral concern for the sick, the transition from Church-related hospitals to municipal or nondenominational hospitals tended to de-emphasize the role of the clergy. Individual ministers were welcome to call on their parishioners, but a general program of ministry was frequently not considered feasible. How could a hospital impartially accommodate the wishes of many denominations to provide religious ministry to the whole hospital? Councils of churches began organizing committees, distributing responsibility for pastoral calling, and arranging for various clergymen to take turns in conducting worship services. But it took some time before many great hospitals actually included a chaplain in the health team, with official status on the staff and payroll.

The necessity of ministering to the sick is not decreasing because of the wonderful advances in medicine. On the contrary, there are more and more people in hospitals because of increases in facilities, better detection of diseases, and public health laws encouraging and providing for hospitalization, as well as increasing age spread in the population. Because people live longer, they can contract a wider range of illness, especially from the chronic group. This increases the number of patient days in the hospital and the number of persons needing spiritual as well as medical care.

Councils of churches and other groups and Church denominations are sponsoring chaplains in hospitals and institutions of great metropolitan areas where thousands of sick people are treated in crowded conditions. Many of these institutions are large communities in themselves, comparable in size to towns and small cities which would have many churches and many full-time clergymen in service. But here in mammoth hospitals we have assembled the condensed suffering of the community. The Government routinely makes provision for chaplaincy service in the large veterans' hospitals just as it does for the Army and Navy. But for the vast majority of patients and hospitals, pastoral care will continue to fall to the parish pastor who is willing and able to provide this ministry.

As clergy and hospital staffs become better acquainted with each other, mutual confidence can be fostered. Former rivalries and jealously guarded professional prerogatives give way to understanding and co-operation. Clinical pastoral training and chaplaincy programs have indirectly aided countless clergymen by developing a receptive attitude on the part of personnel, so that the Church can re-enter the hospital more effectively than ever. Needless to say, parish pastors have also aided chaplaincy programs by their support.

PSYCHOSOMATIC MEDICINE AS A DOOR OPENER AMONG DOCTORS

With greater insight into the psychological implications of illness, there is developing an active, sympathetic interest in mental health on the part of physicians. Jurgen Ruesch has shown that personality maladjustments contribute to the prolonging of chronic illness by making a person a "psychological invalid"; the mind and spirit can cripple the body. (Two convincing presentations in this field are: Jurgen Ruesch and Karl M. Bowman, "Personality and Chronic Illness," *Journal of the American Medical Association,* 136 (1948), pp. 851–855; Jurgen Ruesch, *Chronic Disease and Psychological Invalidism, a Psychosomatic Study,* The American Society for Research in Psychosomatic Problems, 1946.) Flanders Dunbar reports that in many instances of arthritis, emotional factors have damaged the body.

> Arthritis, for example, may be the reaction to a simple emotional problem. It may mask a deeply buried emotional disturbance. It may have created such tissue damage that it is called organic. In all three cases the joints may be equally swollen, the pain equally intense (Flanders Dunbar, *Mind and Body: Psychosomatic Medicine,* Random House, 1947, p. 225).

While the doctor is dealing with the physical results of emotional distress, it is also helpful to have an understanding person listen to and deal with the problems, conflicts, fears, and tensions that are on the patient's heart and mind. Recognition of the emotional factors in illness, together with appreciation of the healing resources to be found in the Christian ministry, can make the pastor a welcome member of the health team and increase the amount of referral made to him.

In psychosomatic medicine, the relationship between mind and body is not being discovered for the first time, but rediscovered and applied to modern situations. In primitive society this close relationship was taken for granted in the fact that the priest and medicine man were the same person. In ancient Greece, Plato made an appeal for a broader concept of medicine.

> So neither ought you to attempt to cure the body without the soul; and this is the reason why the cure of many diseases is unknown to the physicians of Hellas, because they are ignorant of the whole, which ought to be studied also; for the part can never be well unless the whole is well . . . For this is the great error of our day in the treatment of the human body, that physicians separate the soul from the body (B. Jowett, *Dialogues of Plato,* Vol. I, 3d ed., Oxford University Press, 1892, p. 13).

The Greek term *katharsis* is a common psychiatric term today; and the ancient admonition, " Know thyself," has the same goal of self-insight found in modern psychotherapy. These were beginnings; now modern disciplines have systematized and verified these ancient insights into the relation of mind, spirit, or emotions, with the physical well-being of the individual.

Perhaps doctors would not be so willing to open the door for the clergy if medical theory were still confined to the more purely physiological, chemical, or bacteriological frame of reference. Now doctors do not treat obesity as a purely nutritional problem, but are concerned about why people overeat, sometimes to satisfy or compensate for an emotional lack or spiritual hunger. The surgeon is no longer content to bandage or sew up lacerations in a worker who repeatedly injures himself; he seeks also the causes for this " accident proneness," perhaps some anxiety or guilt feelings for which this is an unrealistic solution of self-punishment. Modern medicine is concerned about the whole person and thus naturally overlaps with concerns of religion.

PSYCHOLOGY OF RELIGION AS AN EYE OPENER
FOR CLERGY

The psychological study of religious experience and institutions has contributed to the clergy's interest in pastoral care and counseling. Religion is seen, not only as of theological and doctrinal significance, but also as it pertains to the personality needs of the individual in the crises of life, which he is unable to endure alone, apart from God.

Persons need supportive help during transitions from one stage or mode of life to another. Religion has provided rites of passage to facilitate such transitions in practically every culture, whether primitive or modern. Much has been said about the trauma of birth; the Church provides Baptism as a means of reception into the beloved community, acceptance of the child by the group as well as by God, and supportive approval of the parents in this important event. During the tumultuous time of adolescence, the Church supports the child with group instruction, and announces to all that the child has reached "the age of discretion"; shows its approval through the rite of Confirmation, or some other ceremony of reception into adult membership in the Church, with full spiritual privileges such as the right to receive Holy Communion.

Again, at the time of mature heterosexual adjustment in marriage, the Church gives its blessing in the form of more or less elaborate preparation, ceremonies, and feasting. It is another major transition that the individual goes through, not alone, but with the friendly support of a meaningful group, with the sanction of moral authority, in the presence of God. Many people look to Holy Communion as a strengthening source of stability and restoration in time of failure and sin, trouble and doubt, or sickness. Such crises arise unexpectedly, but with help always available. Death is the final crisis in which the Church stands by the dying person as well as by the family or group that is losing one of its members. If we have not encountered some of the other crises of life, here is one no one can avoid.

To most people, sickness is either a conscious or unconscious crisis, and going to a hospital is a sudden transition during which they need more or less support, depending upon their individual adjustment and situation. This crisis is intensified by the patient's anxiety about his diagnosis and treatment, concern about his family and financial burdens, to say nothing about the physical pains that may attend his entering the hospital. At this point, the Church can be present, in the form of its ordained representative, to stand by and to tide the patient over a difficult period.

Psychology of religion has not only concerned itself with abstract theories, but, lately, especially with the practical relations of physical and mental health to religion. Freud had challenged religion by attributing neuroses to the strictures of religious mores, which caused guilt feelings, repression and frustration of libidinal energy that needed expression. But in the last two or three decades, psychology, psychiatry, social work, and mental health movements have turned to religion to inquire if there were preventive or therapeutic elements in wholesome religious experience. With the advent of psychosomatic medicine and a new appreciation of the importance of emotions in bodily functioning, it is little wonder that psychology of religion has entered this fruitful field of investigation.

There were in Judaism general religious regulations concerned with preventive or public health measures. In the book of Leviticus, Moses provided an elaborate Hebrew sanitary code regarding cleanliness and diet. It showed that the religion of the time was concerned with health. John, in his first Epistle (ch. 3:17), equates good interpersonal relations and altruism with "bowels of compassion" (K.J.V.). Scripture is full of such psychosomatic references, which it is beyond the scope of this work to investigate in detail, but which suggest an awareness of the close interaction between the spirit and bodily changes.

Besides the interest of religion and the Church in healing diseases and caring for the sick by the establishment of hospitals, there is the long history of faith healing from the miracles of the Bible down to the present. This includes the use of holy relics, statues, shrines, pilgrimages, and visions, to which healing powers have been attributed. If space permitted, we should need to include mesmerism, hypnotism, and Christian Science. Some would include psychoanalysis and certain forms of group therapy also under the category of spiritual healing, because they involve spiritual forces such as faith, attitudes, and emotional re-education. Likewise, it would be a fruitful study to analyze spiritual factors of a negative type that aggravate illness or even induce physical breakdown, such as guilt feelings, fear, anger, and grief.

Certainly religion has a great deal to say about how to handle the emotions and attitudes that produce illness. Understood rightly and applied properly, Christianity is able to generate wholesome, constructive emotions and attitudes as well as provide means of dealing with destructive ones. This is especially significant if religious experience is understood to include the unconscious as well as the conscious part of the psyche.

Christianity, viewed psychologically, strives to equip the individual with spiritual resources to meet the stresses of life with faith, hope, and love, and to provide security, purpose, and wholesome interpersonal relations for his life here and now as well as for eternity. Then when failures, sin, tragedy, and conflict come, he can be redeemed from his predicament through God's grace by means of repentance, confession, and forgiveness; he can be healed and accept the realities of life without bitterness or self-pity. Thus the psychological study of religion deepens our understanding of the significance of pastoral care of those sick in body and mind.

With this brief background of the development of pastoral care from antiquity to the present, we need to ask about the present situation of a pastor who seeks to minister to the sick in the modern hospital. With whom must he work and into what combination of services will his efforts fit? Now that we know how and why the pastor found his way into the hospital, let us look at the interprofessional context of his ministry, the health team.

◁ 2 ▷

THE HEALTH TEAM

SPECIALIZATION is a typical characteristic of the average modern hospital. Many intensively trained specialists work side by side, yet are technically unable and legally forbidden to perform the services of other colleagues even in the same department. The health team is this professional group of therapists and technicians who contribute to the care of the patient in the hospital. Because of this multidiscipline approach in the hospital, it is necessary to consider briefly various other roles in the health team, which serves as the professional context in which the pastor works, and into which he must integrate his own role. Among these are the administrator, the doctor, the nurse, the social worker, the occupational therapist, and the dietitian. This is not an exhaustive list, for there are many other significant persons in the therapeutic and social environment of the patient; also the health team varies from one hospital to another depending upon its size, funds, and purpose.

THE ADMINISTRATOR

L. Urwick, in his pioneer work, *Elements of Administration* (Harper & Brothers, 1943, Ch. 1, and especially Fig. 1, p. 19), analyzes administration under three headings: (*a*) The basic *principle* is investigation, research in objectively appraising the situation and determining the appropriateness of the institution in fulfilling the policy of the governing body. Thus the administrator maintains in his own mind and in the semiconsciousness of the institution a principle of order, purpose, or system. (*b*) The process involved is constant forecasting which attempts to answer the question of how needs can be met by the policy already established. Organization arises to execute policy through a chain of command and personnel direction. (*c*) The effect of these first two phases is *planning,* which co-ordinates and controls the process; channeling the activity of the institution is so complex that a group of administrative officers must be set aside to supervise the many departments and numerous workers with impersonal objectivity. Because the administrator is not personally involved in any one particular department, he can view the whole institution with better perspective and consider the functions and needs of the institution as a whole.

The administration is responsible for providing the structure of the health team, clarifying the functions of its various members, and facilitating their relationships in bringing their services to the patient. The administrator and his staff execute the policies determined by the governing body of the hospital, by creating regulations, procedures, rights, and obligations, and making available channels of communication between members of the health team. He also allocates time through scheduling, and material through requisition procedures as well as funds. This aspect of administration could be called group maintenance, the function of maintaining group cohesiveness and unity.

The administrator is in a tension between two processes, both of which necessarily operate simultaneously, the one goal-directed, the other group-directed. Therapy and care of the patient is the general goal of the hospital, but the needs of the members of the health team must also be taken into consideration. For example, in a mental hospital, a certain kind of therapy might be desirable for certain patients, but it might also be so threatening to members of the staff that morale drops to a low level, or some employees resign. In such a hypothetical situation, the administrator would be under pressure to compromise the goal somewhat in order to maintain the hospital as an integral group. It would be extremely difficult for the health team even to exist without some form of administrator.

Goals become institutionalized and standards are set up in order to facilitate the smooth co-operation of various members of the hospital, who may differ personally but yet are able to unite around norms accepted by the whole group. At this point the needs of the individual and the needs of the institution for which he works are mutually satisfied. Paul S. Barrabee speaks of the "institutionalization of goals" as a concept helpful in understanding this mutuality of individual motivation and institutional structure. Thus a norm "utilizes the motivation of the individual to perform an act which will fulfill the functional need of the institution and at the same time it permits the individual to meet a functional need of his own." (*A Study of a Mental Hospital, The Effect of Its Social Structure on Its Functions,* Harvard University, April 2, 1951 [Ph.D. dissertation], pp. 34, 35). In a hospital there must be organizational methods of communicating information pertaining to the goals of the institution and individual responsibility resting upon various members of the institution. As there will never be total agreement on goals and subgoals, nor unanimity as to the best methods of achieving these goals, the administrator makes decisions that are received ambivalently by members of the staff. Barrabee feels this is inherent in his role.

> The foci of the executive's role are on technical competence and on responsibility. . . . In the nature of the case, the executive role is one of the structured foci of the moral and other conflicts of our society, and the executive becomes the recipient of positive and negative affect from the members of the organization (*Ibid.,* pp. 146, 147).

Also there is pressure and judgment brought to bear upon the administrator by the community, which makes him very much aware of public relations as well as internal relations.

How does this role of the administrator affect other members of the health team, and ultimately the care of the patient? The role of authority in making people conform to regulations is often frustrating. Frustration leads to aggression. If morale is low, responsibility not clearly defined, interdepartmental communication slow and sporadic, schedules irregular, and goals in flux, the administrator may be said to be frustrating members of the staff by poor organization. These members of the health team express aggression and hostility against each other and the patients. On the other hand, if responsibility is clearly defined, the staff members feel secure in their rights and obligations; if materials are easily available, schedules regular, and communications available, there is likely to be less aggression because there is less frustration. In the latter case, interprofessional co-operation is fostered and the general emotional tone and social atmosphere of the hospital is more conducive to therapy and care of the patients. The administrator has become an integral part of the health team by facilitating its work in each specialized department, by maintaining the cohesiveness of the group, and by directing its efforts toward the goal of caring for the patient. (For a full discussion of hospital administration see Malcolm T. Mac-Eachern, *Hospital Organization and Management,* Physicians' Record Co., Chicago, 1947.)

Now we shall consider the individual members of the health team, determining their unique roles, in order better to understand the kind of setting in which the chaplain fulfills his role, for he does not work in a social vacuum, nor must he forget the coworkers who care for the patient.

The Doctor

The doctor is considered the leader of the health team in therapy, both in mental and in general hospitals. He heads up departments of specialization, such as internal medicine, surgery, or psychiatry. These various specialities may each have unique meaning, which makes up the difference between the role of the general practitioner or family physician and the role of the doctor in the large hospital. Francis Weld Peabody distinguishes between the two settings:

> Now the essence of the practice of medicine is that it is an intensely personal matter, and one of the chief differences between private practice and hospital practice is that the latter tends to become impersonal (*The Care of the Patient,* Harvard University Press, 1927, p. 12).

In this section we are dealing with the relationship between doctor and patient and other members of the health team in the hospital, yet recognizing that there may be some carry-over of emotional affect and role perception from private office contacts and home visits.

In order to clarify the function of the doctor as a member of the health team, it was helpful to consult one who not only had had broad experience in actual practice, but also was training young doctors to fill this role. Dr. William A. Malamud has provided the writer with helpful insights into this question.

Ideally, there should be one role of the doctor as such, with no need for differentiation between the roles of surgeon, psychiatrist, and general practitioner. But, actually, there is a difference — especially in the higher echelons of the staff. The interns and residents deal with patients as general physicians and represent every specialty. In the higher levels of medicine these functions are specialized, even though each man is still basically a physician. Therefore, they represent different types of functions and have different meanings to the patient. So the surgeon operates and removes organs; the internist examines the heart; and the psychiatrist deals primarily with personality maladjustments. Yet each doctor should be aware enough of the other specialties to be able to make intelligent referral. The reassignment of duties can be a problem if not handled wisely. There is always the problem of rejection, which the patient may feel when transferred from one ward or department of the hospital to another, the feeling that the doctor has lost interest in his case.

The doctor represents the healer. The nurse will carry out the doctor's orders and give regular follow-up care, in a friendly role. But the doctor is the symbol; he represents the healing of disease as such. The symbolic nature of the role of the doctor is augmented by the white coat, the stethoscope hanging from the pocket, and the medical chart in his hand.

But the doctor is also a person. Although patients may react differently to the various functions of surgeon, internist, or psychiatrist, the relationship is very dependent also upon the personality of the doctor and the personality needs of the patient. So the doctor may play the role of father, symbolizing authority, security, and even punishment. The patient can project into the white-coated figure the type of person with whom he needs to relate. The physician communicates his availability for these relationships by his attitudes, behavior, and bedside manner; or he can structure the relationship within very narrow limits as the remover-of-an-organ or the examiner-of-the-heart.

There is not so much likelihood of confusion of roles between the chaplain and surgeon or internist as there may be between the chaplain and psychiatrist in the counseling relationship. Some transference occurs in varying degrees of depth, intensity, and length in every significant interpersonal relationship, whether it be positive or negative. In the pastoral relationship, however, transference in the psychiatric sense is not deliberately sought as a goal in itself. It is relatively an incidental factor. If a chaplain and a patient enter a rather intensive counseling or confessional relationship, this is not to be considered in competition or conflict with the role of the psychiatrist.

The transference situation is a most important relationship between the psychiatrist and the patient, and it does not occur with anyone else to this extent nor for the same purpose. The setting enables the patient to project onto the psychiatrist roles and personalities of various individuals with whom the patient has had important emotional experiences. For example, the person can relive the relationship of playing ball with his father at the age of five or the first experience of being punished. But this delicate material is not allowed to emerge or crystallize by chance. The psychiatrist is able to diagnose the emotional condition of the patient, to judge its severity, and to know what to do about it in therapy. He knows how to direct the relationship into and out of transference so that the patient will be helped and not damaged by the experience. Also, because he is a physician, he is very aware of the patient's physical condition and how organic disorders may be influencing his personality pattern. He becomes a depersonalized symbol in the most intense form when he practices full psychoanalysis and the patient does not even see him as a person in therapy. Here a corollary may be drawn with the Catholic priest, who hears confession behind a screen, with the important difference that the priest does not insist on free association and deals mostly with the present. The chaplain would be definitely outside his role if he attempted to establish and utilize this type of transference relationship in the therapeutic sense without the intensive training that this highly specialized form of therapy requires.

The doctor's role can range from friendly visitor to the authoritative position that unfortunately is forced upon him in the state mental hospital, where he has the " power of the keys " in ordering restrictions or granting freedom. He assumes the role of quasi jailer and judge. This is imposed upon him by the reality factor of the legal situation and the demand of society for a verdict as to the ability of a patient to assume again the responsibility of freedom. This introduces a tremendous emotional reaction on the part of the patient and frequently interferes with treatment. It is possible that the power and authority of the doctor to discharge a patient or keep him longer may have the same meaning in a large general hospital. The doctor is the one who must terminate the security-giving period of " hospitalitis " for the chronic patient and send him back to the harsh realities of the world. Or he is the one who prolongs the separation of man and wife, parent and child, keeping the worker from his gainful employment and thereby attracting the hostility of the latter as much as in the case of the " psychological invalid."

The doctor, per se, often symbolizes authority, security, or healing as well as the interpersonal relationships that exist between himself and the patient. Because of his leadership of the group, he is often a key person in utilizing or ignoring the other members of the health team through referral.

THE NURSE

The nurse carries out the orders of the doctor. Even in the smallest hospital where all the therapies known to modern medicine were not available, there would always be this minimum team of doctor and nurse caring for the patient. Again it seemed advisable to go for information on the role of the nurse in the health team directly to someone in the field, who served as a nurse both in the institutional and public health field, and who was also training persons to occupy the role of nurse. The writer is indebted to Miss Anna C. Gring, Professor of Nursing at the Boston University School of Nursing, for the following insights into the role of the nurse.

The nurse has a familiar role today, and often the first contact with the nurse is in prenatal care and instruction of the expectant mother in clinics. From birth, through early checkups, until the child meets the school nurse in routine examinations, the pattern of " nurse " is clearly enough established so that young children play the role of " nurse " with remarkable accuracy. Increasing use of nurses is being made in industry and other areas of life so that nearly everyone has formed attitudes about nurses before coming into a hospital.

The peculiar role of the nurse is in the giving of intimate physical care in a diversity of situations. This is almost unique, except in the examinations of the doctor. In following the doctor's orders, she administers medications and gives general bedside care to the patients, including baths, injections, feeding, general supervision of the ward, and similar functions generally agreed upon as part of the nurse's role. The intensity of her work with a patient depends partly upon the seriousness of his illness, which may range from critical unconsciousness to convalescent cases where the patient takes almost complete care of himself and may even help with minor tasks around the ward. The nurse's duties vary, depending upon specialization, from operating room assistance and pediatric, obstetric, or orthopedic work, to general ward duty. Whether the nursing is done during the day or night has special connotation and meaning, both as to activity and intensity.

Of all the members of the health team, the nurse is perhaps the most available around the clock. She has a more continuous relationship with the patient than any other member of the health team because she is in and out of the various rooms for an eight-hour stretch, whereas the doctor may see the patient once a day or less, depending on the case. For this reason she often functions on levels and in roles for which she is not officially accredited. If a patient wants to tell an emotionally involved story of home problems at 2:00 A.M. to the night nurse, he does so, not because he does not realize that the social worker could serve in the capacity of a good listener, but because the nurse is available when he is in the mood to talk. Others on the health team often associate the nurse only with physical care, overlooking some of these broader interpersonal roles.

This availability may get the nurse involved with other roles, yet even in areas where she is qualified there is reluctance to use her in any but stereotyped services of physical care. The preparation of the registered nurse includes many insights into personal dynamics and emotional aspects of the patient, yet even psychiatric nurses (until recently) were considered as givers of physical care. One of the personal and professional qualifications of a nurse is to be able to be a good listener. The social worker is also supposed to be a good professional listener. When professional functions and differences have not been resolved in an institution, there are strained and inhibited relationships leading to tension between roles. The chaplain may often feel that when the patient could always bring a problem to him, why has he told it to the nurse? The chaplain may have been available officially, but the nurse was practically available.

Interprofessional conflicts arise when members of the health team are insecure or poorly trained, do not understand each other's roles, or draw too heavily upon their role to satisfy neurotic personal needs at the expense of the goal of the group. For example, a doctor may feel that this is " his " patient in an overly possessive manner. A doctor can be disturbed by an employer seeking to arrange nursing care which may be legitimately included under his compensation plan. These psychological factors operating to mold interpersonal and interprofessional relationships influence the role of the nurse through expectation, limitation, and referral.

Referral is an intricate process about which it is not safe to generalize. It may lead the patient farther from help and away from the particular person who can give it because this service does not fall into his role technically. Perhaps there was a special reason why the above-mentioned patient told the nurse at 2:00 A.M. about his problem, instead of the social worker, chaplain, or psychiatrist. Arbitrary referral may have closed even that already functioning counseling procedure. The nurse can be utilized to interpret many of the personality dynamics she observes from day to day so as to make more effective the work of other members of the health team through understanding referral.

The nurse's function as interpreter is part of the broader role of the nurse, which may or may not be utilized by other therapists. Doctors and ministers will seldom call in the nurse as an active interpreter of the patient's dynamics, whereas they rather frequently refer to the social worker. But the nurse learns much about the patient's economics, family relations, and problems related to health. The nurse may know of a conflict over planned parenthood before the confessor priest or chaplain, and she is able to relate this to other marriage problems and stresses relating to the illness. The function of the interpreter derives its role frequently from a nurse's more intimate association with the total family.

As in the case of the doctor, there are symbolic meanings that a patient may read into the role of the nurse. A nurse is often aware that she is a mother figure for some patient even while the patient himself may be unaware of it. Her own recognition depends upon the background, training, and insight of the individual nurse. A certain amount of dependency on the part of the sick person is to be expected, varying with the degree of actual incapacity. A psychologically well-orientated nurse can sense when this dependency is too intense or lasts for too long a time for the patient's own good. Physical care can mean that mother is taking care of me, so I don't need to take care of myself. Then, on the other hand, painful procedures may symbolize that a parent or other authoritative person is punishing the patient. As a symbol of authority on the ward, with certain administrative prerogatives and reporting to the doctor on the patient's condition and behavior, the nurse is likely to be the recipient of some hostility. The extent to which she can handle and understand such negative reactions on the part of patients will determine partly how much she is able to fulfill the broader role of the nurse in caring for the whole patient.

Further observations on the role of the nurse in relation to the role of the chaplain will be made in a later section, based upon the data gathered from interviews and questionnaires for nurses.

THE MEDICAL SOCIAL WORKER

It is interesting that the same man, Dr. Richard Cabot, who encouraged ministers to become members of the health team by having a clinical year in a hospital as part of their theological education, was also a pioneer in bringing the social worker into the staff of the hospital. Both these roles, that of the chaplain and of the social worker, are nonmedical in the sense that they do not give any physical treatment. But wherein do their functions differ, and what is the role of the social worker? Again, the most direct approach seemed to be to confer with one who is training people to fill this role in the hospital. Mrs. Ruth Cowin, Faculty Supervisor of Medical Social Work and teacher of the course "Medical Social Case Work" in the Boston University School of Social Work, kindly helped to clarify the role of the social worker. The writer is indebted to her for the following material.

The general background of social work students before specializing in hospital work is nonauthoritative. In the general agency in the community the majority of cases are self-referred. The client must want help herself in order to be accepted, for the type of help the agency has to offer cannot be forced upon a person. Even when a third party, such as employer, pastor, or relative, makes referral, the social worker tries to be sure that there is full willingness on the part of the client to participate and come for interviews. Only an agency like the Society for Prevention of Cruelty to Children comes in unsolicited, sent by the police, the court, or an anonymous complaint. So in the specialized field of medical social work there needs to be a change of orientation. This involves the basic question of authority.

In the hospital setting, authority is often appropriate, as in the situation of a child, a delirious patient or one that is unconscious, a patient who is psychotic, or one who is senile or deteriorated. At such points the hospital assumes that medical urgency or public safety (as in the cases of contagious disease) justifies the use of relative degrees of authority. Different members of the health team use authority, and in the multidiscipline approach of the hospital there is often the question of who should use it, how much, and when. The doctor is the authority because of his expertness and knowledge of what is best for the patient, as well as because of the need for a leader of the therapy group. The nurse is also authoritative when she stands by the bedside while the patient swallows the pill and then reports to the doctor whether or not the patient accepted the treatment or medicine. So in the midst of this institutional setting, the patient does not understand nonauthoritative roles. The patient will ask the social worker, "Do I have to do this?" And it is only after interpretation that the patient discovers that the social worker is not primarily a manipulator of the environment or a giver of social orders. The social worker must recognize and handle this problem of authority, not only in working with the patients, but also in relationships with others on the staff.

In a sense the patient is self-referred to the hospital, and it may be assumed, ideally at least, that the patient is willing to receive whatever treatment and facilities the hospital has to offer. The functions of the social worker correspond generally to the functions of the hospital, and the primary reason for her being there is individual service to the patient. Adequate referral helps facilitate the role of the social worker. But often the doctor refers without consultation with the patient and without explanation. Then she comes upon the scene as a surprise to the patient. This puts upon the social worker the need to justify herself in being there.

As the social worker has become integrated into the team and demonstrated her value, clinical services have begun to appreciate the influence and the importance of emotional, social, and psychological factors in the causation of disease and the patient's response to treatment. Physical and psychological rest are influenced by simple environmental factors of everyday life over which the patient may be worrying and also by complex emotional problems. This is especially appreciated when the staff is aware of the psychosomatic approach to illness.

Doctors are the primary source of referral to social workers, with nurses second. Chaplains are often aware of the need to refer patients, and sometimes the patients themselves request service because they have heard of another patient on the ward who was helped. Relatives also make requests for service, and the administration may call upon a social worker in problems of finance, posthospital care, or admission. Sometimes there is a one hundred per cent review of all admissions, as in tuberculosis, mental, or chronic hospitals, where it is usually taken for granted that long hospitalization will create financial and social adjustments beyond the capacity of the average person or family to cope with alone. Whenever anyone other than the doctor makes a referral, the social worker does not take another step until she gets medical authority and checks with the doctor about the physical condition of the patient and the medical program that is prescribed.

Some of the services represented are the following:

1. Transportation of patients to outpatient clinics, where patient is unable to arrange such for himself.
2. Anything helping to make medical care effective, such as talking with the patient about how he feels about his condition and treatments prescribed. Reducing anxiety.
3. Discovering allied problems that may relate to patient's illness or future rehabilitation.
4. Working with other agencies through referral to bring resources of the community and the needs of the patient together, such as needs for medical appliances, braces, or money, because many people find it very difficult to accept such help.
5. In cases of chronic or terminal care, providing or suggesting resources and implementing such help in details.
6. Study of the patient and family in the diagnostic approach to cases of invalidism where patients appear to be overwhelmed by relatively small symptoms.
7. Follow-up of patients in outpatient clinics and later home adjustment, making referral to other appropriate agencies when problem goes beyond the limitations assigned to the social worker of the hospital.

In spite of the extensive service of the medical social worker, the patient often does not consider her an integral member of the staff. He may ask, " Whom do you work for? " or, " Are you from the welfare department? " Partly this is due to the attitude of the administration as it is interpreted in budgets and bills. The patient is not billed by most hospitals for professional services rendered by the social service department as he is for laboratory work done and X-ray. Yet some hospitals are beginning to make this kind of formal recognition of social service.

Confidentiality of case records is used because the social worker is a part of the health team. There is no danger where there seems to be overlapping if social worker and chaplain are secure in their own roles. Two criteria are (1) whomever the patient selects, and (2) whoever is there first.

In conclusion, the functions of the social worker may be grouped under four headings: (1) Service to patients; (2) Teaching of social work students-in-training; (3) Research in her field; (4) Preventive programs of mental hygiene. Counseling with other staff members should be kept on the informal basis and not emphasized too much.

The Occupational Therapist

The place of the occupational therapist on the health team has been demonstrated especially during the recent wars since the problem of rehabilitation has been acute. Her services range from direct physical effect of exercise and muscle-building movements to the psychological value of making articles which demonstrate to the patient himself and others that he is improving or at least useful — hence the term "therapy through occupation." The doctors are likely to utilize this resource in proportion as they have seen that it has contributed to the goal of the entire health team, namely, recovery or care of the patient. Miss Marion W. Easton, who is Director of Clinical Training in the Boston School of Occupational Therapy, is registered both as an occupational therapist and a physical therapist. It was felt that she would be a good resource to describe the role of the occupational therapist. The following is material based upon her comments.

The occupational therapist works directly under the medical supervision of the doctor in carrying out the aim of treatment of the patient. Her function is as broad as the facilities of the hospital and her own ingenuity allow. Mental and physical resources are used to motivate the patient to do his part in his recovery. In this area of treatment, the patient must carry it out, whereas in physical therapy, for example, the treatment is done either for or to the patient. It is like a sugar-coated pill. The sugar-coating is the interesting activity, whereas the medicine inside is the specific need being ministered to with the therapy. The end product (the article made) is what the patient has his attention focused on, but it is not the main thing. With physical illness, the effects are direct and the therapy prescribed is given to the patient so that he knows what the aim is and why the approach is more indirect. For example, the overexcited mental patient may be given the task of breaking up boxes in the occupational therapy shop so that the wood can be used for projects. In reality the purpose is to give the patient opportunity to work off his aggression. Or he may be assigned the occupation of working in the steam laundry in a monotonous, repetitive work, for its sedative effects. One of the difficulties in occupational therapy is to know why some effects or results take place. In purely physical treatment the results are more tangible and concrete. Treatment may thus be *functional* — applied to a definite physical function of part of the body, or *psychological* — so that the patient loses himself in some prescribed activity.

The role of the occupational therapist may vary greatly, especially in a mental hospital. It is not always what the therapist chooses, but what the doctor assigns to suit the needs of the patient. So the occupational therapist may be asked to take the part of the mother with one patient and the sister with another. This is indirect psychotherapy. She is channeling the patient's interests while other members of the health team are looking for the root of his disability or illness. She is considered a person who is interested in helping the patient to help himself.

In the Army hospital, the occupational therapists served first as civilian employees without uniform. This helped the patients to feel at home with the therapists and consider them as links with the world outside the institution. The therapist could often give much information to the doctors that the patients would not share with staff members more closely identified with the hospital and Army regimen. Even in the Navy, where the occupational therapist was an officer wearing the uniform, the servicemen somehow felt that he was a civilian at heart.

The aims of the occupational therapist fall roughly under four headings: physical, mental, social-adjustment, and economic.

1. Physical aims necessitate selecting an activity that will improve joint motion, increase muscle strength and work tolerance, and develop co-ordination. Here a wide variety of activities are available to suit each individual disability.

2. Mental aims include raising the general morale of the patient so that he may derive the optimum benefit from his hospitalization. An attempt is made to help him adjust to his illness, to alleviate the mental stress, induce relaxation, or stimulate interest and motivation as is needed in each case. Generally the purpose and aim is to estab-

lish as normal a day as possible, which would include work, play, rest, and sleep. Choice of work programs, active and passive recreation depend on the staff and their ingenuity.

3. Social adjustment is broader than the mental aim because it brings into play the forces of interpersonal relationships, helping the patient to fit into the social life of the hospital and subsequently into his own social groups after leaving the hospital.

4. Economic aims of occupational therapy seek to make the patient as independent as his capacity will permit, both in the family household and in the economy of the community. For many patients, the test of their own recovery is when they are economically rehabilitated and able in some degree to turn out useful work.

The activities used to achieve these goals and aims are extremely varied and numerous. Referrals should be specific, but often much is left to the discretion of the occupational therapist. Four general types of activities are used, namely: manual, recreational, prevocational, and educational.

1. Manual activities stimulate the creative interests of the patient in producing a completed article through media of woodworking, metal crafts, leatherwork, etc. This is perhaps the most common conception of occupational therapy.

2. Recreational activities include games, sports, programs, movies, singing and dancing, etc., which combine physical, mental, and social aims at the same time.

3. Prevocational activities test the skills, aptitudes, and interests of the patient to help to readjust him to a realistic level of rehabilitation and find for himself his place in society. At this point there is close co-operation and referral to vocational guidance resources.

4. Educational activities include helping patients with correspondence courses, typing, and other projects, so that the patient will not feel that time spent in the hospital has been wasted. This phase would be of special importance in persons whose education is interrupted, and the occupational therapist's part would depend partly upon whether there were special teachers on the staff of the hospital. This is an indication of how far the field of occupational therapy has progressed beyond the hooked-rug and woven-basket stage.

Still, of 122 activities used (according to a survey), the 5 major activities are still weaving, cord-knotting, leatherwork, woodworking, and art work. The question is whether or not administrations make only these facilities available and expect these activities to be done, or whether these are the activities therapists are best trained to use. The administrator has an important role in utilizing occupational therapy, and he must want the department and interpret it to the rest of the staff if it is to be of optimum value.

Occupational therapy, especially in diversional types of activity, utilizes volunteers, and thus the therapists are freed for more specialized work. This aspect depends upon the location of the hospital, its accessibility to a large community and transportation facilities, and the attitude of the administration toward volunteers. They should be screened, guided, and used properly, in order to obtain the maximum service for the patients and also give the volunteers the feeling of usefulness and achievement. Such volunteers are often a valuable link between the hospital and the community at large in the public relations sense.

The writer knows of three mental hospitals where clinical pastoral training is closely tied up with the occupational therapy department. Through this channel the students make contact with the patients in both a service and a learning capacity. They are the Boston State, Boston Psychopathic, and Worcester State Hospitals in Massachusetts. Because of its broad implications, it is useful for the chaplain to be aware of the role of the occupational therapist in the total care of his patient.

THE DIETITIAN

As an indication of how the health team may vary, depending upon the individual needs of the patients, the work of the dietitian will be cited. Just as in the case of tuberculosis there would be frequent contact with the X-ray technician, so in the case of diabetes, the dietitian would be a significant therapist. The same would hold true of feeding and weight control problems. O. Spurgeon English, who is a well-known figure in the field of psychosomatic medicine, feels that a more significant place comparable to that accorded to social workers, occupational therapists, and nurses, should be given to the dietitian as a member of the health team. This is useful and suggestive as to how members of the health team could ideally be used more than they are. The problem is to be aware of and utilize the resources that various therapists have to offer, and this must be recognized especially by the doctor, who is the head of the team and often so preoccupied with his own role that he does not have time to be aware of the possibilities inherent in other roles. English suggests three practical services that the dietitian could render:

(1) Gain information (a social and dietary history) which would be valuable in treating the patient and which the physician rarely has time to collect. . . .

(2) Under the physician's directions . . . enter into the therapeutic situation and help to modify faulty attitudes.

(3) Give support to a dietary regimen which requires frequent contacts and the presence of a feminine and/or maternal figure and supply a much-needed interest in the patient's welfare. In convalescence, for instance, there is a tendency for all patients to regress to a varying degree to childlike feeling, and the " woman " who is interested in what the patient eats can have a great deal to do with peace of mind as well as the will to get well (" The Role of the Dietitian," *Journal of the American Dietetic Association,* Vol. 27, No. 9, 1951, p. 724).

These are illuminating suggestions showing the dynamic nature of a role that is often thought of in the minimum stereotype as a combination cook and waitress. This discussion is not descriptive of what the role is in most hospitals, but what it could be at the optimum.

At Simmons College, Boston, there is a program for training dietitians to work in hospitals, under the department of Home Economics. Dr. Elda Robb, who is the head of this department and professor in this field, kindly gave of her time to clarify for the writer the role of the dietitian in the hospital as she has seen it.

The role of the dietitian is as one of a team, especially in the outpatient or food clinic. At the Boston Dispensary, both in the diabetic clinic and weight-control class, the dietitian plays an important part. Unfortunately the dietitian often means deprivation of food in reducing and special diets. She receives the hostility of the patient even if it is the doctor who prescribes the diet. Food means more to a person when he is sick; in the hospital he looks forward to meals, especially if the food is good and the patient fairly well. If the patient realizes that food is an important factor in his recovery, e.g., in diabetes, than it is a positive relationship. She may be more often with the patient than the doctor. In the best hospitals she has personal contact with the patients.

But reality factors sometimes keep her away from the patients. Food is the second largest item in the hospital budget, so there is the management of much money, which takes a lot of time. And supervision of the kitchen has priority because, whatever else is done, the food must be prepared three times a day, and in time.

Nevertheless, personal contact with patients is what motivates many women to go into the field of hospital dietetics. Out of 16 students in the institutional management course, in dietetics at Simmons, 10 are planning on entering the hospital field. Men who enter food production work go into the competitive field commercially, while women go into the hospital work. There seems to be an appeal in the "hospital" setting for women. It involves taking care of sick people and appeals to the maternal instinct. Therefore, dietetics does not just mean food to these women, but food in the care of the patient. If this is missing, they leave the hospital field and often go into public health work, where they get more personal contact with people. Ideally, the dietitian should be part of the team working closely with the social worker and the psychiatric departments. But often she is not sensitive enough to the psychiatric aspects of food problems, when the problem is more than just food. Some doctors have begun to train dietitians and have consequently utilized dietitians more. This is especially true when the hospital is affiliated with a medical school and is a teaching hospital. The full-fledged member of the American Dietetic Association has had four years of college and one year in an approved internship.

The role of the dietitian is illustrative of many other similar service departments which can be very meaningful to the patient, depending upon his particular illness and need. Similar discussions could be made about the medical technician, who would be a frequent visitor to the bedside of patients who were having many special tests involving blood samples, etc. Other technicians take cardiograms, encephalograms, give insulin or electric shock treatments, all of which have various meanings to different patients ranging from, " I'm just another case going through the mill," to, " They're doing all they can for me; I've been taking tests all week." All this discussion about the various roles of members of the health team indicates what a complex concept the " health team " is, varying from one hospital to another and surely from patient to patient. No one member should feel disappointed if he is not the key figure in the care of one patient, because in another instance his contribution may be the crucial service.

To indicate that all this therapy does not take place in a social vacuum, it is necessary to suggest that there are many meaningful and significant persons who are in contact with the patient, such as visitors, relatives, janitors, ward aides, volunteers, as well as other patients in the same room or corridor. These persons may have a beneficial or harmful effect upon the patient's progress. The hospital sometimes has less control over these persons than over the official therapists.

The Chaplain in the Health Team
OR
Seeing Ourselves as Others See Us

The role of the chaplain in the care of the patient is relatively new in many hospitals. In the health team, as in any group, it takes time and experimentation before the status of a new member becomes clear and secure. In exploring the status of the role of the chaplain, it was considered necessary to go directly to hospital chaplains for data, by means of interviews and by questionnaires. (Material for this section is drawn from a Ph.D. dissertation by the author entitled, *The Role of the Chaplain in the Care of the Patient,* Boston University, 1952.) The sample of chaplains was drawn from the Chaplains' Section of the American Protestant Hospital Association. Out of 45 accredited, active chaplains, 39 co-operated in this study. They represented 10 Protestant denominations and came from 8 different states. An attempt was made to reach 2 doctors, 2 nurses, and 2 patients with whom each chaplain had worked closely. Table I shows the number of persons in each category reached by interviews and questionnaires.

Table I

SAMPLE OF SUBJECTS INCLUDED IN THE STUDY
WITH METHODS USED TO OBTAIN THE DATA

Method	Chaplains	Doctors	Nurses	Patients	Total
Interviews	18	25	32	22	97
Questionnaires	21	26	29	23	99
Total	39	51	61	45	196

The role concept is useful in delineating the interpersonal relationships of group dynamics. In the case of the chaplaincy, the significant interprofessional group and social context for the role of the chaplain is the health team, or staff of the hospital.

The doctors can either utilize or ignore the pastoral resources of the chaplain. If they have found such services helpful and therapeutic in the care of the patients in the past, they will make referral to the chaplain and seek to include him in the health team. Likewise, if a doctor is personally hostile to religion or has had unfortunate experiences with clergymen in the past, the chaplain may very effectively be kept outside of the health team even though he is officially listed on the staff of the hospital.

The opinions and role perceptions of nurses are influential in determining the degree of integration of the chaplain's role into the health team. Being in close contact with patients many hours a day, they can make patients available to the chaplain and the chaplain available to the patients. However, if their opinions of the function and services of the chaplain are vastly different from his perception of his role, naturally he cannot serve as the chaplain in the given area.

The object of the efforts of the health team has not yet been mentioned, namely, the patient. If chaplain, doctor, and nurse all agree that the chaplain can be of help to a given patient in a certain area (such as religious counseling), but if the patient should refuse to accept the chaplain in that role, the chaplain cannot function on the health team in that particular capacity.

The chaplain functions with increasing effectiveness to the extent that other significant persons share a similar perception of his role. For example, 59 per cent of the doctors, 51 per cent of the nurses, 49 per cent of the chaplains, and 42 per cent of the patients mentioned religious counseling as a unique function of the chaplain; this shows agreement of role perception. All four groups expect and accept it to about the same degree when responding to the open-ended question, "What aspects of the chaplain's work are most unique, i.e., could be performed only by the chaplain?"

There was a wide disparity of opinion about religious acts, such as sacraments, prayer, and Scripture-reading. Thirty-one per cent of the chaplains, only 4 per cent of the doctors, 21 per cent of the nurses, and 39 per cent of the patients mentioned this factor as being most frequently requested of the chaplain. Thus, there may be more effective role fulfillment in the area of religious counseling than in the area of religious acts because there is more agreement in role perception in the former while lack of agreement in the latter allows only partial role fulfillment.

To illustrate how four different persons might view the role or function of the chaplain, Figure 1 is presented. Each person's conception or perception of the chaplaincy is represented by an egg-shaped form. Obviously the forms are not the same size or shape because no two persons have identical perceptions of a task or service; each one sees it from his own biased frame of reference.

The doctor has had quite different training and sometimes has different value judgments from the pastor. The nurse is like the doctor in her appreciation of medical procedures, but brings a feminine point of view to her role perception. The patient is outside the health team, a transient guest who may not have the vaguest idea of what kind of service the chaplain could possibly render to him, or he may have a clear idea of just when and why he would call for the chaplain's ministry. Obviously the chaplain has put most thought on just what is involved in his role, when he should be sent for, how he can help patients in various situations, and how the rest of the staff should relate to him.

Where there is no overlapping of opinion, the spaces are white, as in D and C. This represents attitudes and role perception peculiar or unique to that one person. Sometimes two persons see things eye

RELATIONSHIPS OF FOUR PERCEPTIONS
OF THE ROLE OF THE CHAPLAIN

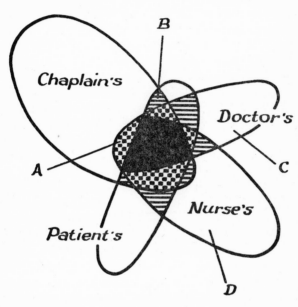

Key

☐ Perception unique to one

☰ Perception shared by two

▦ Perception shared by three

■ Perception shared by four

to eye, and a striped area is indicated as in B. The checkered area, indicated by the latter A, shows that chaplain, doctor, and nurse agree that the chaplain could render a special service to the patient, but the patient is either unaware of it or disagrees. The solid black area in the center indicates functions of the chaplain's role upon which all four are agreed. In this last instance, the chaplain has the best chance of really fulfilling his ministry. The more complete and intense the integration of the chaplain's role into the health team the larger will be the proportion of the diagram that is black, indicating clear and mutual understanding of his function and acceptance of his ministry.

In attempting to discover sources and forms of resistance to the chaplain from other members of the staff, it appeared that lack of clarity of the role of the chaplain accounted for the second largest number of responses, 35 per cent. (Forty-two per cent of the responses indicated direct hostility, personal resentments, or conflicts against the chaplain, usually of a personal nature rather than emphasizing his role.) The chaplain's role is sometimes unclear to other staff members so that they do not know what to expect of him, how he is to function, or when and how to refer to him. This negative communication could be modified greatly by the chaplain's taking the initiative to interpret his role to other members of the health team. Sixty-four per cent of the responses stated that there was no resistance.

Several factors make this element of resistance to including the chaplain on the health team a difficult one to analyze. The chaplain may not be aware of hostility when it exists. Other staff members may hesitate to show and express hostility toward the chaplain because of his clerical status or for some other reason. Another difficulty involved is in interpreting what is and what is not an expression of hostility or resistance when responses are made to open-ended questions. There is need for further research on this question of resistance and hostility, not only in the case of the chaplain but against clergymen, per se. No doubt the usual stereotype of the authoritarian figure of the clergyman is often a symbol of inhibition and frustration, which quite naturally tends to create aggression and hostility. Perhaps the chaplain is the recipient of hostility unconsciously intended for the administrator or other authoritative figures in the institution, such as head nurses or the department heads.

In order to ascertain the criteria by which the chaplain's role was judged to be an integral part of the staff by doctors, nurses, patients, and chaplains themselves, the following question was asked: "How do you consider the chaplain an integral member of the staff? Illustrate by a typical example. To what was such status in the institution attributed?" Interestingly, 68 per cent of the chaplains felt themselves to be considered integral members of the staff; 16 per cent answered that they were not considered an integral part of the hospital staff; and 16 per cent were ambivalent, or stated that they were uncertain at this point.

After analyzing all the responses of chaplains, doctors, nurses, and patients, it appeared that status on the staff for the chaplain was judged on the basis of the following four factors: (1) *Administration:* symbols of administrative sanction, authority, or responsibility, such as office space, use of official channels of communication, prerogatives, status as a department head, access to the director, modes of reporting, etc. (2) *Other staff:* the opinion or attitude of other staff members, approval of doctors and nurses, to be acknowledged together with other staff members who are obviously and securely on the team, such as doctors or nurses, or being considered a professional equal of other staff members in any way. (3) *Therapy:* the direct result of the chaplain's work with patients showing therapeutic significance, tangible evidence of professional competence in counseling and pastoral care. (4) *Clergy:* factors pertaining to the clergy, per se, as representing the Church, religion, aspects of the role perception related to the role of the "clergyman," whether in the hospital setting or in the community at large.

Chaplains considered themselves to be integral members of the staff in the following ways: Administration — 25 per cent; Other staff — 42 per cent; Therapy — 39 per cent; Clergy — 8 per cent. This tends to indicate that chaplains lean heavily upon the opinions and esteem of other staff members who have a secure status and whose role is clearly defined. This would naturally be expected if the role of the chaplain is to attain *dependent integration* with the health team. Almost an equal percentage of chaplains relied upon their actual work with patients as a criterion for their integration into the staff. This is a sign of greater security, i.e., to depend upon one's own merit and inherent usefulness and effectiveness. This might be referred to as *earned integration*. Administration could be considered *attributed integration;* it is given by fiat (although in some cases it may have been earned or bargained for). Status due to merely being a clergyman was not listed by many chaplains and may be considered *professional integration;* i.e., the role has a status accepted in its own right, regardless of the purpose or goal of the various groups concerned.

The role of the chaplain needs to be integrated into the health team by interpretation and clarification of his functions and by interprofessional co-operation and mutual respect. Interpretation is important because communication between the chaplain and others on the staff is dependent upon their perception of his role. The chaplain who has earned integration into the health team of his hospital and who shares his perceptions of his role with the largest number of significant people is the one who functions most effectively in the role of the chaplain in the care of the patient.

It is in this rich professional and social interaction that the chaplain works and into which he must integrate his pastoral services and role if he is to be accepted as a member of the health team. He needs to interpret his role to the administrator, doctor, nurse, and any other significant persons in the hospital, so that they may know how he can be used most effectively and what his relationship is to others on the staff. The chaplain does not function as an isolated worker with an individual patient. The admission clerk, doctor, and nurse have very likely seen the patient before the chaplain has contact with him; and following the chaplain's call there may be treatments given in various departments, visits from relatives, conversation with fellow patients (sometimes in reference to the chaplain's visit), and repeated contacts with the nurse. The purpose of this chapter on the health team has been to suggest the complex pattern of interprofessional and interpersonal relations in which the chaplain fulfills his role in the care of the patient.

◁ 3 ▷

RESOURCES OF THE PASTOR

ANY professional worker becomes more effective as he recognizes the full potentialities of the resources available to him. The teacher who omits audio-visual aids is limiting the opportunities for maximum learning efficiency. A doctor would not think of neglecting X-ray, blood tests, and other appropriate diagnostic aids as resources for making decisions. He knows that for possible treatment he can resort to surgery, medication, rest, heat, or changes in diet. What, then, are the resources of the pastor? Often the pastor wishes he could walk into the patient's room with as concrete a set of resources as the physician's little black bag, administer an injection, record the exact temperature, and leave a prescription. But his resources are often less tangible, and this may increase his desire to " do something " and to feel that he is of immediate and specific help.

INTERPERSONAL RELATIONSHIPS

Relationships are a fundamental concern of Christianity and therefore of the pastor. At the center of the universe is God, the Person who is above all concerned that his creatures live in a close relationship with him so that he can bless them with an abundant life. Throughout the history of the Hebrew people and the Jewish nation, he was concerned that the covenant relationship should not be broken, and sent prophets to urge both the people as a whole and individuals to return to this relationship. When the Messiah finally came, he sought to bridge the gap that separated man from God and restore the unifying divine relationship. John records the high-priestly prayer of Christ (in the seventeenth chapter of his Gospel) in which this is especially evident: " I do not pray for these only, but also for those who are to believe in me through their word, that they may all be one; even as thou, Father, art in me, and I in thee, that they also may be in us, so that the world may believe that thou has sent me. The glory which thou hast given me I have given to them, that they may be one even as we are one, I in them and thou in me, that they may become perfectly one."

The oft-repeated desire or goal of the Christian life is to live with Christ and the Heavenly Father, not only during this life in the flesh but in all eternity. No wonder the importance of relationships has always been apparent in pastoral care, and, interestingly enough, is being rediscovered and studied by contemporary social psychology.

The pastor has not only the relationship of the counseling situation as a resource, but, as a representative of the Church, he has perhaps more ready-formed therapy groups than any other professional worker in the community. There is the local parish, within which a person may find groups to meet his need of establishing meaningful relationships, not only with God, but also with people of like interests and needs. When the patient leaves the hospital, he can be related to some such resource for abundant living as membership in the Christian fellowship. Many church groups will accept a stranger as a member of a warm family and provide that necessary security of " belonging " that so many neurotic, lonely people lack. A church group is a resource for pastoral care only when it is an accepting, friendly, nonthreatening group. The church needs to develop such groups to support discharged patients (especially those re-entering the community after a stay in a mental or penal institution). By his symbolic role, the pastor reminds the patient of familiar group relationships in his home environment, whether it is a Sunday school class, the youth group, the women's or men's group, or the Sunday morning worship group and the parish as a whole.

In the pastoral counseling there has been a shift from dependence upon authority and tradition to more reliance on a warm, secure interpersonal relationship between pastor and parishioner as the foundation for emotional growth and the finding of solutions to problems. Exhortation, advice, and suggestion are all more or less

present in authoritarian relationships. Fifty years ago there was mor(
confidence in the conscious and intellectual faculties of man. The
pastor felt that his main task was to appeal to reason in giving
advice, point out several reasons why the parishioner was in his
predicament, and show two or three logical steps to be taken in solv-
ing his problem. This method was used in social agencies also, but is
now considered one of the outmoded methods. (Carl R. Rogers,
Counseling and Psychotherapy, Houghton Mifflin Company, 1942.
See Ch. II, " Old and New Viewpoints.") Newer concepts in pastoral psychology and counseling turn the attention away from the
counselor toward the counselee and his feelings and needs. The
parishioner or patient is the center of such counseling rather than
the cleverness or the authority of the pastor. This is a difficult shift
of role for many pastors to make as they try to adapt themselves to
this newer method of work with individuals and become concerned
about the interpersonal relationship in the counseling process. There
have been many traditional counselors who used these methods in-
tuitively, such as the intimate family doctor, the friendly old priest,
or the patient, understanding pastor, but only recently has there
been a conscious and formal attempt to state and follow these psychological principles in the method of counseling.

The pastoral relationship, because of its traditional and symbolic
nature, includes and connotes much more than the momentary interpersonal relationship of two persons during the pastoral call or
counseling situation; it also includes the associations the counselee
has with religion, authority, and early experiences in developing
moral attitudes as well as the present moral sanctions inherent in
the Church. So, in " Pastor Jones," there are also overtones of God
the Father, as well as childhood association with " Daddy." In Ca-
tholicism this is accentuated by calling the priest " Father," but even
where the title " Mister " is used of the clergy, the psychological implications and associations may be equally potent, depending upon
the individual's religious background.

Harry Stack Sullivan describes the symbolic nature of the relationship between psychiatrist and patient as follows:

> Besides the two-group integrated of psychiatrist and subject there
> is in the parataxic situations also an illusory two-group integrated

of psychiatrist-distorted-to-accommodate-a-special-'you' pattern and subject-reliving-an-earlier-unresolved-integration-and-manifesting-the-corresponding-special-'me' pattern (*Conceptions of Modern Psychiatry*. The William Alanson White Psychiatric Foundation, 1940, Washington, D.C. Reprinted in 1947 with addition of "Critical Appraisal of the Theory," by Patrick Mullahy).

While this concept complicates the counseling relationship beyond the ability of the average pastor to comprehend its psychiatric implications, it is useful in showing how forceful the role of counselor is in arousing associations and memories of other significant relationships. When the chaplain meets a patient in the hospital, he has to cope not only with the present relationship, but there accrue unto him all (or at least many) of the former associations with clergymen, whether they have been frustrating, punitive, supportive, permissive, bigoted, or tolerant. Jung's exploration of the collective unconscious has bearing on this point, because there is also the culturally accepted stereotype which is placed over the pastoral office and which has an influence upon the pastoral relationship at the unconscious level, even if it is not admitted (or in some cases consciously rejected) by the pastor, the patient, or both.

It is important for the pastor to structure the relationship as clearly as possible and at the same time be sensitive to whether the patient is accepting this relationship and what it means to him. Charles F. Kemp discusses this symbolic role of the pastor.

His role and function as a minister have been, through centuries of Christian culture, bred into the deeper levels of the consciousness of those whom he serves. Therefore he has symbolic as well as personal influence, and the symbolic power of his role gives him a strength far beyond that of his own personal appeal to people (*Physicians of the Soul,* The Macmillan Company, 1947, p. 26).

The element of "levels of the consciousness" should also include "unconscious" areas of the personality from which deep speaks unto deep. The pastor's "strength far beyond that of his own personal appeal to people" should not be considered an unadulterated blessing. In some cases it will be a strength, in others an inhibitor and repressive factor so great as to prevent even elementary communication because of the emotional blocks against " pastor " per se. Oftentimes, by not pushing the role of pastor or chaplain upon a resistant patient, but by showing friendly, nonthreatening interest in the patient as a person, the chaplain is able to break down these barriers and earn the right to be the person's pastor in spite of the handicap of the patient's former inadequate relationships with other pastors. The burden of structuring the pastoral relationship rests largely upon the chaplain. This is usually best done by a genuine empathetic concern for the patient as an individual, and ability to respond accurately to his emotional and spiritual needs. Once this relationship has been clarified and established, the patient is invited to utilize it as he has need.

Yet this section should not end with the impression that pastoral counseling is the only relationship involved in the work of either the parish pastor or the hospital chaplain. Dean Walter G. Muelder, of the Boston University School of Theology, has said that the minister is " the most general practitioner of all the professions." He " has to play a great many roles that other professions do not have to play. But he has to know what role he is playing and why " (From a lecture on " The Role of the Minister " given at Massachusetts General Hospital, Boston, August 24, 1951). Thus he is preacher, educator, priest, administrator, etc., as well as pastoral counselor, depending upon whether he is in the pulpit, teaching a class in Church history in the Sunday school, administering the Holy Communion, presiding at a board meeting, or being sought out in his study by a person in distress. But he must keep these roles clear for himself and others, so that he does not preach in the counseling situation nor hope to accomplish most of his administrative function from the pulpit. Also, he must understand the distinction between his role as counselor, when supposedly the patient is receiving the major attention, and his social relationships, wherein the pastor is having his own personal needs met. Even here the relationship is often confused, because a pastor may have entered upon his work in order to satisfy many basic, yet unrecognized, needs of his own, and it may be difficult to say who is receiving the most benefit from the pastoral relationship.

Finally, there is the intricate problem of the intensity or depth suitable for the pastoral relationship, which may range from a level comparable to psychoanalytic depth therapy to the repressive-inspirational type of group meeting. (See J. W. Klapman for a description of the various levels of psychotherapy, *Group Psychotherapy,* New York, Grune & Stratton, Inc., 1946, pp. 68–71.) It is necessary for the pastor to be aware of the level on which the transference or communication is taking place and whether or not he has the understanding and techniques for handling the relationship. William Brown gives a good admonition at this point to the overly eager pastoral counselor:

> What, then, remains for the clergyman to do? If the clergyman feels a special call to deal with psychoneurotic cases, he should certainly get analyzed himself and learn all he can about analysis, and although he may not have the opportunity of applying it, he should bear the facts in mind and apply them, and, when he deals with patients, take care not to be dogmatic (*Personality and Religion,* University of London Press, 1946, p. 83).

A good rule is not to encourage any relationship in pastoral care or counseling for which one is not willing to accept responsibility for the consequences. In other words, if the level of the problem is too deep, make referral to another member of the health team, a psychiatrist, or social agency. The pastor must define this role for himself and not drift or be pushed into counseling relationships that he cannot handle. There is nothing like a tragic suicide or a murder to convince a pastor that he should have shared responsibility with some other skilled therapist through referral.

We have seen from the above that interpersonal relationships comprise one of the most fundamental resources of the pastor in his work with the sick. He must understand the significance and dynamics of such relationships and know how and when to utilize them. This will help him not only to avoid many blunders but also to understand his patients better.

SCRIPTURE AND DEVOTIONAL LITERATURE

Scripture is another resource that has various meanings for different patients. Some consider it primarily as an uncompromising book of law, containing the Ten Commandments and other authoritarian dicta on what to do and what not to do. Their earliest recollections of Scripture may be painful memories of stage fright while trying to recite some obscure passage in a Sunday school Christmas program, which may not have helped their already deep-rooted feelings of inferiority. Another patient brings his Bible with him to the hospital as a source of comfort and strength, finding in it the forgiveness of God and the love of his Saviour. Perhaps in the background of this person's experience are memories of a loving mother and father who read from the Bible in the midst of a secure family circle. These contrasting examples illustrate how the chaplain cannot assume that he knows what the Scripture means to any given patient without some understanding of that person's attitude and background. Spiritual resources may not necessarily have the same significance for the patient as for the chaplain.

The Bible deals with many specific issues and problems of life such as sin, guilt, family relations, sibling rivalry, the nature of God and his will for man's life, etc. Naturally, the various passages and stories of Scripture need to be used appropriately. If a patient believes that he has committed the " unpardonable sin " and is utterly beyond the scope of God's love, he does not need further proof from the prophets of how much God hates sin; he needs to discover that God is an all-loving and merciful, forgiving Father. By identification with many characters in Scriptural accounts, the doubter can see himself in Thomas, the adulterer in David, and the physically ill in Job. By projecting himself into their situation, the patient can believe that if God helped and forgave and saved these sinners, there is also hope for himself in a similar situation.

Frequently, a patient will ask a seemingly academic question about some Biblical character such as Job; but underneath lies the implicit question, " Why did this happen to *me?* " Therefore, the Bible should not be used mechanically, nor administered as an injection of just so many verses at random, but rather with an alert awareness of the patient's needs and what the Biblical reference might mean for him. Then it is recognized as a living and relevant word of God to him in his individual need.

There are excellent supplements to Bible-reading that have been especially designed for the sick. These should not be distributed wholesale any more than the doctor would order a dozen pills to be passed out indiscriminately to all the patients in the hospital. Religious tracts must be carefully screened and scrutinized because, unfortunately, much of the material is inadequate theology and harmful from a mental hygiene point of view. No doubt some people feel that when a person is trapped in a hospital bed and confronted with a serious crisis, the time is ripe for a " decision." We need to consider the ethical implications of the " captive audience " concept in performing our pastoral care of the sick. Chaplains frequently must undo the damage done by careless use of coercive, threatening, and unscriptural devotional literature.

On the other hand, there is a large quantity of both theologically and psychologically sound devotional literature available. Such aids lend themselves to use by patients for seven reasons according to Chaplain Malcolm B. Ballinger, of University Hospital, Ann Arbor, Michigan: (1) It is symbolic of Christian faith. (2) It is tangible, " capable of being touched." (3) It is available when needed by the patient. (4) It can direct the thinking and feeling of the patient when he may be too listless to direct himself. (5) Good devotional literature can answer some questions and help the patient accept his situation and himself. (6) He can share his pamphlet with others, which helps foster interpersonal relations. (7) It may help the patient verbalize his feelings to the chaplain (" Devotional Literature for Patients," *Bulletin of the American Protestant Hospital Association,* April, 1951).

In choosing devotional literature, as well as passages of Scripture to read, consider the patient's needs, how he may interpret the content, and the appropriate goals for this patient's future. At various times a patient may need to be supported in crisis, helped to express himself, comforted in tragedy, strengthened in his faith, aided in finding a purpose for living, provided with a larger vision and assurance of God's providence, love, and personal concern for each individual.

Also the capacity of the patient must be considered; physical, mental, educational, and spiritual. How heavy a book can an arthritic patient hold in her painful hands? Can the elderly person read the small print of some editions of the Bible? Not everyone has the intellectual capacity to follow the subtle nuances of devotional pamphlets designed for college students. Vocabulary is an important factor and can be a source of frustration if above the level of the reader. The church member from a pietistic background likes the warm, personal approach, whereas another may appreciate a logically reasoned and objective emphasis, even to the point of asking for some theological books about certain doctrines of the Church. Be alert to the wide range of devotional and religious literature that can be helpful for patients of different types.

Scripture and devotional literature can perpetuate and foster pastoral care between the chaplain's calls as well as during them.

PRAYER AND FAITH

Prayer and faith are closely related. The writer has frequently heard patients say that they find it hard to pray because God seems so far away and their faith in him so weak. The opposite effect is also possible: faith in God becomes weaker if we cut off communications with him through lack of prayer. James (Ch. 5:15) combines both in the verse already referred to: " And the prayer of faith will save the sick man."

The Church teaches that faith in God is an essential foundation upon which to build the personality structure; it is the core from which motivation, attitudes, and behavior should radiate. In discussing the nature of conversion, William James wrote:

> Let us hereafter, in speaking of the hot place in a man's consciousness, the group of ideas to which he devotes himself, and from which he works, call it the *habitual center of his personal energy* (*The Varieties of Religious Experience.* Random House, 1902, p. 193).

Among believers, this faith-center of life is a great resource, of which the pastor can take cognizance in a unique way.

Other counselors can help a patient with his neurotic feelings through catharsis and a permissive attitude, as well as clarify the various alternative courses of action from which the counselee can choose. Psychoanalysis, for example, is effective in unraveling the complex skein of human emotions and forgotten experiences; but a criticism (especially leveled at the earlier theories of Freud) is that it does not devote enough attention to the core of life around which the loose ends of thread can be rewound. Yet many psychiatrists and secular counselors recognize this need of "a purpose for life," "something to live for," "a reason for my existence," and sometimes make a referral to a hospital chaplain to help the patient find this needed pillar of strength and guiding, directive force called "faith."

A woman patient in a hospital had confessed a grievous series of mistakes and sins to the psychotherapist, but somehow this catharsis was not enough. She could not believe that things could ever be all right again, that she could be accepted again. The therapist, in an earnest effort to demonstrate his acceptance of her, said, "But I understand; I forgive you." The woman replied, "You can't forgive my sins; only God could do that." The physician referred her to the chaplain and told him that he would have to help her find this forgiveness, which later she did find.

The Christian faith gives not only a reason for why we are here, for the source of life, and for the significance of life through the doctrine of creation; it also provides a foundation for forgiveness through the doctrine of the atonement and Christ's redemption. A patient who believes that God is also continuously concerned enough about his life to send his Holy Spirit as a comforter, guide, and sanctifier has a strong resource with which to meet life's situations. The pastor should remember that among many patients this resource of faith is a factor on which he can count; among others it must be generated and strengthened.

Gordon W. Allport, a modern psychologist with a keen appreciation for the importance of a faith as a "unifying philosophy of life," has this to say about the psychological and supportive role of religious belief as a unique resource:

> Religion is the search for a value underlying *all* things, and as such is the most comprehensive of all the possible philosophies of life. A deeply moving religious experience is not readily forgotten, but is likely to remain as a focus of thought and desire. Many lives have no such focus; for them religion is an indifferent matter, or else a purely formal and compartmental interest. But the authenti-

cally religious personality unites the tangible present with some comprehensive views of the world that makes this tangible present intelligible and acceptable to him. Psychotherapy recognizes this integrative function of religion in personality, soundness of mind being aided by the possession of a completely embracing theory of life (*Personality: A Psychological Interpretation,* Henry Holt & Co., 1937, p. 226).

This "focus" or experience of faith may be the result of a sudden conversion or the outgrowth of long years of Christian education, but in either case it is a unique resource of pastoral care of the sick, frequently a rallying point for revitalized mental and physical health.

Although faith is a necessary support for all of a person's life, it becomes more obviously important in times of great crisis, disappointment, and, of course, death. Paul E. Johnson states, "When he confronts such alternatives of life against death, the first need of a man is to believe . . . the Christian hypothesis that life can survive death" (*Psychology of Pastoral Care,* Abingdon Press, 1953, p. 256). Not only for the dying believer, but also for the bereaved, belief in eternal life, the resurrection, and a loving Father God supports them in an otherwise unbearable crisis. Thus faith and hope combine to supply the necessary direction and goal of life; pain and loss can be better borne in this larger perspective which gives meaning to life.

Faith is a resource the pastor cannot share unless he possesses it himself. Richard C. Cabot and Russell L. Dicks stress this fundamental prerequisite and obligation:

The minister's duty there [in the sickroom] is to rouse the great energies, certainties, and faiths of the Christian religion. If he has Christian faith, and otherwise he has no business in the ministry, he has a great asset, perhaps the greatest asset a person could have in dealing with the sick. His peculiar privilege springs from the fact that he has a living and sometimes a contagious belief in God, in immortality, and in the soul's endless power for growth (*The Art of Ministering to the Sick,* The Macmillan Company, 1936, p. 5).

The pastor communicates this faith, not only by words, but also by attitudes and actions; not only by talking about the peace and love of God, but also by demonstrating it as a current experience. Often the patient will make his own statement of faith and trust in God if the pastor will only listen and give him a chance to express himself. Faith is dynamic and real when it is actually his own experience and not something administered secondhand. For some the affirmation of their faith in the words of the Apostles' Creed provides a meaningful reassurance in familiar terms.

Prayer is a traditional resource of the pastor. Just as a child cries out for help to parents, so it is that a patient in the stressful hospital situation is likely to become more aware of his dependence upon God and pray to him for help, whether it be for immediate cure or spiritual strength to undergo the crisis. The patient may resent this tendency as a childish regression or be ashamed to pray to God for help now when he never turned to him in years of health and prosperity. This resource calls for careful discretion on the part of the pastor.

The patient may actually be requesting the chaplain to line up God on his side against the doctor by saying (or thinking), " Please pray for me that I won't have that second operation," while actually the patient is in the midst of a two-stage operation which requires a ten-day convalescence before the second stage can be completed. It is often useful to precede prayer with a permissive and exploratory conversation. " What would you like us to pray about? " or some such approach may help clarify the patient's thinking and feeling and make prayer more meaningful than if the chaplain proceeds without understanding the patient's frame of mind.

There is great cathartic value in prayers for forgiveness if the patient has been able to verbalize feelings of guilt and repentance. A formal statement of absolution and benediction can give added assurance to the penitent, but should not be made prematurely as it can also serve as a repressive factor. In other words, care must be taken not to cut the patient off in the midst of his confession or verbalization of his problem; this could prevent him from sharing the rest of his burden or make him feel that only this amount could be accepted by the pastor as well as by God. The patient can tell from the chaplain's prayer whether or not he understands him and his numerous worries, otherwise the prayer may be vain repetition and superficial platitudes. It is possible to force him into a hypocritical position by putting words into his mouth that are not in his heart. Imagine the gulf between pastor and parishioner if the former is glibly praying in terms of gratitude for God's bountiful blessings and thanksgivings for his mercy and the latter is quite sure he has nothing to be thankful for.

In prayer, as in the use of other pastoral resources, one can be best guided by concentrating on the needs and feelings of the patient and trying to put oneself in his place.

Silence and meditation should not be overlooked in connection with prayer. Every moment does not have to be filled with the noise and chatter of spoken conversation to avoid embarrassing silences. The quiet meditation of two believers in the presence of God can sometimes deepen one's spiritual sensitivity, a calm expectation that God is communicating also in a two-way relationship. The writer has often seen such moments of quiet bear more fruit than conversation ever could have at that particular time. Let us surround prayer with a quiet, unhurried atmosphere and the calm confidence of faith in God.

SACRAMENTS AND SYMBOLISM

The sacraments are a tangible means of grace, a resource that can be grasped with the senses as well as by the abstract thoughts of the mind. The very touching, tasting, smelling, and swallowing involved in the Holy Communion re-enforce the idea of forgiveness from God. The concept becomes an action, and what may formerly have been a promise now becomes personal experience.

The Holy Communion must be used and administered in an understanding manner, being mindful of the background of the patient and its meaning to him. Some patients may consider an invitation to the Lord's Supper as a preparation for death and a sure sign that the doctor is withholding the dread information from him, but nevertheless sending the pastor to prepare him for the inevitable. Another patient, accustomed to receiving Communion regularly, will be inclined to welcome it. The latter will not only experience a closer fellowship with God but also share in the " Communion of saints," since his relatives and friends in the home parish may also be participating in the same experience. This bond of unity in the faith is especially meaningful to one who feels deeply the loneliness and isolation of hospital confinement, the uncertainty of the progress of his disease, and the sufferings of his illness.

Again timing is important. When a patient requests Communion, time spent in talking it over will be well spent. What significance does the sacrament have for the patient at this time? Has he always received Communion on the first Sunday of the month in his own church? Does he ask for this in connection with some crisis, before an operation, upon learning of his diagnosis, or after a series of rather intensive counseling sessions in which he has unburdened himself of many sins and guilt feelings?

Make sure the nurse knows when Communion will be administered so that she can prevent interruption. Co-operation is usually easily secured if asked for courteously in advance. Make sure the patient knows what is going to happen. Prepare an appropriate setting in view of the patient so he can see what is being done.

This leads to the matter of the use of symbolism in connection with pastoral care. At the University Hospital in Ann Arbor, Michigan, Chaplain Ballinger has found it useful to leave an upright wooden cross on the bedside table of selected patients whom he knows will appreciate it. This visual reminder of the Christian faith continues the chaplain's pastoral care even between his visits much the same as does devotional literature. A weak patient who cannot read can at least look at the cross. Especially during the administration of the Holy Communion, a cross will be a meaningful symbol upon the bedside table.

What of symbolism to identify the pastor himself? Identification of each class of worker in modern hospitals is routine. A unique uniform is worn by doctors, workers, occupational therapists, Gray Ladies, etc. Many chaplains, therefore, find it necessary and useful to identify themselves with equal clarity by wearing clerical garb or a white or gray jacket with a cross pinned or embroidered on it in a conspicuous place. Frequently clinical training students find that such a mark of one's role makes introductions easier and minimizes interruptions by other personnel who might otherwise mistake the student for another visitor.

Some pastors and students are fearful that such marks of identification will create a barrier by emphasizing status and setting oneself apart as " different." However, an essential in pastoral care or counseling is to structure the relationship and to define the limits of the relationship so that the patient or client will not expect services or opportunities that are not possible. The theological student who discovers that the patient has thought for fifteen minutes of a call that she was talking to the medical resident on the floor will desire to identify himself more clearly in the future.

Each pastor or student has to evaluate this matter in light of his own tradition, personal background, and feelings. Clerical garb, as well as other evidences of status and authority, can be worn appropriately and effectively or can be carried about as a defense mechanism and an attempt to make up for feelings of personal insecurity. Symbols are most effective when used with a sense of naturalness and appropriateness.

WORSHIP AND GROUP METHODS

The worship service on Sunday is often the highlight of the patient's week and a common method of pastoral ministry where a chaplain or council of churches has arranged for such opportunities in co-operation with the administration. At this point one needs to recognize the limitations of space, housekeeping facilities, and personnel, and should be thoughtful of the workers in order to foster a wholesome attitude toward such services on the part of the staff. After all, when such a program is begun, it will entail extra work for the staff to escort and wheel patients from the wards to the chapel, prepare the room, etc. Sometimes willing volunteers can be found to assist in such tasks.

While serving as chaplain at the Robert B. Brigham Hospital in Boston, the writer designed a combination altar and bookcase of the same size as the opening of the fireplace in the day room (which served also as a lounge, party room, and medical conference room). A drape was hung above the fireplace as a dossal to cover a secular frieze. When the altar was wheeled into place with cross and candles on top, a worship center was created with minimum effort. During the week the back of this piece of furniture served as a book-

case in the corner of the day room, containing devotional literature and materials needed for the services. Arthritic patients had
made the cross and candlesticks in the occupational therapy department, and also printed the bulletins on a hand press in that department. Folding chairs were set up on one side of the room, while the
other side was left clear for wheel chairs or beds to be rolled in.

Within the same hospital other groups were created for informal
discussions of topics of mutual concern. These topics can range from
group-chosen subjects to a series about great Biblical characters,
preferably within a permissive framework. Patients not only gain
the benefits of " belonging " to a group of other people in the same
situation but can also express their concerns and share their feelings,
which they might otherwise have to keep pent up inside. Such
group leadership requires an accepting attitude and the capacity of
the leader to minimize his own participation and encourage others
to take part. Such informal groups provide a good supplement to
the formal or liturgical worship services.

Groups from local churches can reach out and extend their influence to patients who are temporarily (or permanently) isolated
from their natural group memberships. Church groups that are
looking for social service opportunities can be sources of volunteer
workers in the hospital, and, with supervision, may be helpful visitors. Boston State Hospital, through the contacts of Chaplain Robert
Leslie, has been served by many church groups who sponsor ward
parties, send cards and gifts at Christmas and other times, and in
various ways help substitute for the group memberships of which
patients are deprived during hospitalization. All such efforts should
be cleared carefully through the administration and medical and
nursing staffs.

Groups focusing their combined attention upon worship and
communion with God, hearing the Scriptures read, and singing
hymns together, or sharing their feelings in free discussion, can all
serve as valuable resources in the pastoral care of the sick.

Steps Along the Way of Salvation

Many theological concepts take on new meaning when we see
them in the light of pastoral care of someone in distress. These in-

sights will be listed here in the sequence sometimes referred to as the *"ordo salutis"*:

Sin is frequently defined in terms acceptable to each generation, e.g.: our generation prefers to speak of "inadequate interpersonal relations," "antisocial behavior," "hostility," "actions in conflict with the superego," etc. Whatever we want to call such breakdown, or as the Bible says, "missing the mark," modern medicine recognizes these as directly related to health and illness through a rediscovery of psychosomatic medicine. Therefore, when a patient tells the chaplain that he is maybe suffering because of something he has done or thought, the chaplain does not brush it off and try to console him with a hasty reassurance that he needn't worry about it. Rather, he will wait for him to clarify his feelings further. At this very point comes the diagnostic test of reality; guilt feelings for having committed some sin against his wife or neighbor are not only realistic but the first step toward a solution — the pain that urges one to seek a solution. But if this guilt feeling is unrealistic or inappropriate, then there is indication that the source is not known to the patient; he does not know the origin of his problem. This is true of the anxious neurotic who does not find relief no matter how many times he confesses his "sin"; actually he has not been talking about the right thing. The pastor should not hesitate to discuss sin when a patient brings it up for fear it will be bad pastoral psychology. For further light on this topic we need to turn to another age-old concept.

Repentance is a person's reaction to his sin when he has laid aside the various defense mechanisms and rationalizations that people usually use to protect the ego from the truth. He admits his failure and faults and assumes responsibility for his actions and their consequences. How can the pastor encourage such honesty and self-examination? Usually people who have gotten into trouble are not unaware of the facts of morality. They know intellectually that it is not best to desert one's wife and children, lose one's fortune through chronic alcoholism, worry one's self into an ulcer over a business promotion, hate one's parents, etc. Their problem is to accept this emotionally as well as intellectually. Deep down they have not dared to admit error, for to do so would be to lose face, to go down in defeat. Yet this is essential before any real work on the problem can begin. Social case workers and psychotherapists would call this a " felt need." The pastor can encourage this more effectively by indicating that he would understand how people can have troubles and failures than by a further emphasis on the facts of morality that the patient already knows intellectually. But once this attitude of a felt need is present, what then?

Confession is the historic term for verbalizing one's sense of guilt, telling one's problem to a trusted confidant, sharing this sense of repentance, and seeking a solution and release from the unbearable situation. The pastor can facilitate this much needed step by simply being an accepting, understanding listener, by making it clear that all that is confessed wil be held in strict confidence, and by withholding judgment and condemnation. A patient or parishioner will often begin with a small part of his confessional story to see how the pastor takes it. Will he be shocked, indignant, amused, threatened, vindictive, hurt, or judgmental? If the pastor is any of these, the confession will no doubt terminate, and the poor person in need of help and forgiveness will have to look elsewhere for a true pastor, a more adequate shepherd of souls.

The healing of the soul, and sometimes even of the body, begins in this stage of cleansing, which psychologists call " catharsis." Just as a physical wound must be thoroughly cleansed before a bandage can be applied, so the spiritual sore spot must be cleansed of all negative, destructive, and harmful elements. This process cannot be hurried or forced. The best way to make sure that the patient is receiving the maximum benefit from this spiritual self-examination is to let him go at his own speed and say what is on his heart and mind in his own words. It is a real temptation for the pastor to want to put appropriate and stereotyped words into his mouth, but this is artificial and encourages hypocrisy. Next we come to the goal of this confession.

Forgiveness is possible only on the part of a loving and accepting God, and it is likewise possible on the part of those in whom this love of God abides. A Christian minister must have a heavy endowment of this gift of grace if he is to reveal and demonstrate and express this forgiveness and acceptance when once the confession has brought out many unseemly and morbid facts of failure, sin, and defeat. What a tragedy in instances where a pastor has a neurotic need to be vindictive and punitive toward the helpless penitent who has now bared his sin-sick soul! And what a relief to the troubled person who at last has an understanding pastor with whom he has found it safe to share his troubles. To this person absolution becomes more than a mere formula of words; in fact, it is superfluous to say the words because it is so apparent and obvious that forgiveness has been experienced.

Every pastor will have thought through the doctrine of atonement in the course of his theological education. Such basic matters of systematic theology are taken for granted in this book and their detailed treatment is beyond the scope of this work. But it is important to emphasize the necessity for a consistent approach on the part of the pastor so that his theology and his methods of pastoral care do not work against each other. Perhaps the reader can recall from his own experience some pastor who intellectually affirmed the grace of the gospel, but who almost invariably dealt with people, even penitents, almost exclusively in terms of the law of the Old Testament. That pastor had a conflict between what he thought and how he felt. Perhaps he had accepted grace as an academic position or as a teaching of the Church, but underneath he may have had personal needs to be punitive, judgmental, unaccepting of other people. Obviously, such a pastor is greatly handicapped in trying to help a penitent know and experience the forgiveness of God.

Sanctification, growth in the new-found grace and love of God, is an essential aspect of pastoral care. Once the negative and destructive elements of sin have been rooted out of a person's experience, the impediments to interpersonal relations lessened, the person is now free to move forward constructively to new and more effective living. The energy formerly consumed in a neurotic and anxious attempt to deal with his problems can now be directed toward more wholesome goals. The finding of such goals, and even the initiating of tentative or exploratory efforts to arrive at such goals, is the final stage of the counseling process. The pastor must be concerned about helping the patient or parishioner through the beginnings of this stage of his spiritual struggle. Jesus emphasized the danger of leaving the house clean yet empty after having driven the devil out. There can be a false sense of security and relief after having undergone the difficult and painful ordeal of self-examination and confession. New goals and ambitions must be decided upon by the counselee that will not lead him into the problems from which he has so recently been untangled. These new goals must be realistic, appropriate, and ones to which he can commit himself fully with his new understanding of the Christian life.

Here, again, the pastor will be tempted to superimpose his goals upon the counselee or patient. These are not nearly so likely to be helpful or lasting as those which the person discovers and sees for himself. How natural it seems for the pastor to want to say, " If I were in your place, I'd move to another city and get a new job," or, " Since all this trouble started from living with your wife's parents, I suggest that you and your wife find an apartment of your own across town "! Such advice can very easily rob the person of the spiritual birthright of choosing his own goals and living his own life. It also makes him dependent upon the pastor for future decisions. Surely one of the hopes of this pastoral relationship has been to help the person to grow and mature, to acquire and develop the inner resources necessary for dealing with life situations. Granted, there may be times when an especially weak person needs a bit more support in his fearful reaching out for new goals before he dares to act upon his decision, but let this be the exception rather than the rule.

One of the advantages of pastoral counseling over other forms of counseling is the continual follow-up available through the normal pastoral care of the parish life even after the formal counseling relationship has been terminated. The pastor can still give mild support through pastoral calls in the home, seeing the person in the worship services, and relating him to groups within the church. (Such referral has already been mentioned in the case of a hospital chaplain.) The pastor helps the patient or counselee to see his past problem in the light of future goals and actions, not only in this life but also in the perspective of eternity. Many other counselors do not feel free to go as far as this. Dedicating oneself to the Kingdom of God, to some great cause within the Church, or to a specific service of someone else in need, can provide worthy satisfactions for life to replace the former inadequate and harmful ones derived from a neurotic need.

All these pastoral resources, which are here considered primarily from a counseling point of view, also contribute to the Christian education of the parishioner or counselee, for, as surely as he has learned how to deal with his present problem and need, he will know how to approach other crises and where to turn for help. He will also have experienced a new understanding of the nature and will of God, a better understanding of himself and his destiny.

◁ 4 ▷

THE PASTORAL CALL

Many factors besides the conversation with the patient help to determine the effectiveness of a pastoral call in a hospital. Since many hospitals are complex institutions, the pastor must first make his way through a maze of information clerks, corridors, nurses' stations, etc. (without stepping on toes), before he finally arrives at the patient's room. He must size up the situation and the patient in an intuitive glance before he is ready to introduce himself. The appropriateness of various pastoral resources must be evaluated as the call progresses and suitable termination decided upon by the pastor. Throughout all this process, he must have remained primarily concerned about the patient as an individual and not think of him as just another name on his list.

Making Sure that the Way Is Clear

As a pastor enters the average hospital, he needs to be aware that he is standing with one foot in each of two distinct social institutions: the Church and the hospital. The fact that both these elements of society are well-structured institutions has certain implications for his work. To use a mechanical illustration, two cogwheels must mesh gears smoothly in order to accomplish a useful function. In Chapter 1, a great change was noted. Whereas, at one time the hospital was part of the Church, now the Church is asking to be allowed to be part of the hospital through pastoral services and chaplaincy programs.

An institution that has relinquished some of its functions to another may tend to become very defensive as it feels its strength or influence declining. Therefore, clergymen need to guard against becoming defensive in the presence of the medical staff and in their domain. The parish pastor would do well to consider himself a guest in the hospital until he has been given indication that he is considered a member of the professional family. He should show appreciation for all courtesies extended to clergymen and earn the staff's confidence and acceptance of him by considerate co-operation with all personnel and observance of all rules of the hospital.

Regulations and restrictions generally have some rationale behind them, whether they are based on therapeutic benefits for the patients, convenience for the personnel in executing their various functions, or the economic requirements of budgetary limitations. The pastor who barges into the hospital and insists on his "rights," regardless of the concerns of the hospital staff, will not receive a warm welcome or maximum co-operation. He would do much better to look upon his entry into the hospital as a privilege and try to make his calls fit into the complex pattern of hospital activities. Therefore, he should try to avoid mealtime, the early hours when medications, baths, and other services are administered to patients, and other times that he might discover are inappropriate. Speaking to the staff about the best time to call will indicate to them that he is taking their convenience and experience into account. Since he is doing his part, they will be more willing to accommodate him when he needs special favors or assistance (such as helping to provide privacy for individual Communion services).

Attribute to each staff member or worker the proper status of that position. Do not ask the nurses' aide questions about policy which should be directed to the head nurse on the floor. On the other hand, questions of diagnosis and prognosis and discharge should generally be directed to the doctor instead of the nurse. Suggestions made by doctors and nurses should be taken into careful consideration. They may have information about the patient's condition or situation that makes their opinions a real contribution. The pastoral caller should go out of his way to make sure that the patient is available for a visit and go through the proper channels to find out, generally by asking the nurse at the ward station.

KNOWING THE PATIENT

To most people, sickness is either a conscious or an unconscious threat, and going to the hospital is a great transition. The pastor cannot know what this experience means to the patient immediately, but he can try to see things from the patient's point of view as much as possible. Dr. Francis Peabody indicates something of the patient's frame of reference in the following picturesque description, showing the drastic change from " well person " to " patient status ":

> Here, for instance, is a poor fellow who has just been jolted to the hospital in an ambulance. A string of questions about himself and his family has been fired at him, his valuables and even his clothes have been taken away from him, and he is wheeled into the ward on a truck, miserable, scared, defenseless, and, in his nakedness, unable to run away. He is lifted into a bed, becomes conscious of the fact that he is the center of interest in the ward, wishes that he had stayed at home among friends, and, just as he is beginning to take stock of his surroundings, finds that a thermometer is being stuck under his tongue. It is all strange and new, and he wonders what is going to happen to him next (*The Care of the Patient,* Harvard University Press, 1927, p. 37).

The pastoral caller should not take for granted that he knows what hospitalization means to any given patient. To one woman with hypochondriacal tendencies, being sick and running up large hospital and doctor bills was the only effective means she had discovered of punishing her husband for his mistakes and lack of consideration. To another patient, hospitalization might mean security: all his basic needs are cared for, he is bathed, fed, told when to go to sleep and when to wake up (this is especially true in mental hospitals). The farmer is quite justifiably anxious about being hospitalized at the beginning of the crucial harvest season, and every routine examination seems a needless delay. Some attitudes of the patients are " normal " and reasonable; others are based upon motives and feelings and fears that are buried far below the surface and not discerned by an untrained observer. Many previous experiences with illness and doctors, or stories and rumors about operations and other people's experiences in the hospital, color the patient's attitude toward his hospitalization.

How, then, can the pastor " know the patient " if he cannot take for granted the " normal " communications of the patient? Perhaps the key here is patience. The temptation is to try to hurry the process of getting acquainted because of the shortness of time. Yet no one can get to know a person (patient or otherwise) faster than that person wants to reveal himself. Deeper feelings and thoughts are revealed (especially to a stranger) only when it seems relatively safe to do so, only after an accepting, understanding relationship has been established.

In the process of getting to know the patient, the pastor must forget himself, his special and immediate interests, his own interpretations of what this patient's experience in the hospital would mean to himself, and he must concentrate on putting himself in the patient's shoes, on listening to the patient's story, on trying to feel the way he feels about anything the patient chooses to share with him during the call. This is more than sympathy (feeling *with* a person); this is empathy (feeling *into* his experience and situation).

The pastor must sacrifice his own ego needs temporarily, abandoning himself to the other person's needs. He must set aside his own problems temporarily in order to absorb another's problems, concerns, pains, conflicts, joys, aspirations, successes, and failures. This is essential before the pastor can really begin to know the patient in a dynamic and meaningful way. Such an approach does not specify certain techniques and steps as much as it is an attitude toward the patient, a willingness to be available, to listen and be ready to share when invited. Before the pastor is ready to render any specific pastoral service, he needs to know, as one student wrote on his report, " who and where the patient is."

ESTABLISHING AND CLARIFYING THE PASTORAL RELATIONSHIP

Relationship as a pastoral resource was discussed in the previous chapter. Yet one may agree that this is important without knowing how to go about establishing this unique kind of relationship. Quite frequently the patient has a great many interpersonal relationships — neighbors, parents, cousins, social friends, intimate friends, plus some enemies — but he may lack, and desperately need, a creative relationship, a permissive, therapeutic opportunity to relate to someone who has not prejudged him, taken sides in his conflicts, or determined his goals for him. The pastor, then, is not just another friend or relative. Friends are usually too much involved, having pretty well made up their minds what course a person should follow, to be of therapeutic usefulness as counselors. The pastor can come as a neutral, as a detached third party, and bring the benefits of an objective attitude, thus offering a new dimension, an opportunity to approach the problem afresh.

A pastor once wondered why none of the teen-age boys with whom he worked very closely ever brought their personal problems (which he learned about from other sources) to him. He played games with them frequently and tried in every way to be their friend, a " buddy," as he put it. That was his handicap: he had become so involved as a friend that he had forfeited his chance to be their pastoral counselor. The boys had enough friends, and their needs were not met by having one more " buddy."

In this sense counseling is different from friendship. In friendship two people can let down their hair to each other. The counselor, however, does not share all his problems with the counselee; in short, it is not truly mutual as among friends. The counselor is available for the benefit of the counselee; if the counselor needs therapy, he should seek another counselor, but not look for his therapy from the present counseling situation with his client or parishioner. In the case of the pastor-patient relationship, the need for clarity is apparent. The pastor can indicate by his attitude and responses that he considers this a patient-centered call. In that sense, this may very well be a unique relationship for the patient, not merely an exchange of news and pleasantries, not even the host-guest relationship in which social amenities and polite entertainment are the main concern. The pastor should leave behind all his own problems about the church budget, the building campaign, the recent slack in attendance at worship, where he'll spend his vacation, etc., when he enters the sickroom. The patient can then feel free to talk about *his* real concerns because he doesn't have to worry about the needs and problems of his " friend."

Before an adequate relationship can be established, the patient must also have a clear idea of "who" the caller is and by what authority he has come into his room (which is his home-away-from-home), what his role is, and the function he can or intends to perform. One theological student made a call on an elderly patient for about ten minutes only to discover at the conclusion of the visit that the patient had mistaken him all the time for the medical intern assigned to that hospital ward. He had not made his role and function clear; it is doubtful if this could be called a pastoral call. The student could have avoided or prevented this by a clear statement such as, "I'm Mr. Brown from the Protestant chaplain's office." If the patient had not caught on, the student should have taken time to clarify this. Perhaps the term "chaplain" is strange to some people, in which case other explanatory terms can be used, such as "hospital pastor," or "minister here in the hospital."

A parish pastor said, "But all my people know me." It's a sad day when a minister calls only on his "own people." The author found from his parish experience that at least half his calls on the sick and shut-in were on nonmembers: unchurched neighbors, in-laws, friends, contacts of members of his congregation. Often it was necessary to clarify at the beginning who he was and where he came from. A simple: "I'm Pastor Smith from Trinity Church. Your cousin Bill Jones told me you had come to the hospital rather unexpectedly," clears away any misgivings or embarrassment that might arise if the patient is left in the dark as to who the visitor is and why he came.

Some students find it difficult to assume the detached role necessary in pastoral counseling or calling and cannot even attribute the title "Mr." or, if ordained, "Pastor," to themselves even though the nurse and doctor and social worker all maintain this professional relationship. They find it easier to be casual and introduce themselves as "Andy Jones" or "Chuck Smith." One clinical pastoral training student, who had previously only thought of himself as a perpetual youth worker, was enabled for the first time to conceive of himself as a pastor of a congregation, really occupying the status and playing the role of a clergyman, through this experience of interpreting and introducing himself to patients in the hospital.

This is a matter of mature, professional self-acceptance. It is hoped that the patients will accept themselves; pastors must also accept themselves.

Once the relationship is well established, there is still the possibility that it will have to be clarified repeatedly. Patients insist that the pastor make decisions for them which can only be made by themselves; e.g.: " Do you think I should have my leg amputated; some doctors say I should, some say I shouldn't? " (need for clarification between doctor's role, pastor's role, and patient's own responsibility for decision); " Do you think I'm eligible for old age assistance? " (need for referral to medical social worker or county welfare worker); or, " Will you please raise my bed up and give me a drink of water? " (perhaps these two simple things might be under nursing supervision — intake of fluids being measured and need for lying perfectly prostrate for some medical reason). In all these cases and many others, the pastor must determine what his role is and thus be responsible for that relationship. In short, he defines the limits and then allows the patient freedom to bring up anything within those limits.

One of the limits is that of time. Some patients would gladly chat away for two or three hours, but frequently the usefulness of the call has reached its maximum by ten or fifteen minutes. It would be more useful to make three shorter calls than one extremely long call in most cases. There is the danger of overfatigue as well as the possibility that, once the floodgates of emotional reserve are opened up, the patient may have misgivings about having told so much on an initial interview. The pastoral caller needs to protect the patient by determining the end of the call at an appropriate place, which naturally has to be evaluated in each call on its own merits. He must also be aware of good stewardship of time and not neglect some by concentrating wholly on the few " interesting cases."

Determining the Appropriateness of Various Resources

One patient reported that she could have screamed as she heard the hospital chaplain coming down the corridor each day, stopping at various rooms and reading his " Scripture for the day." By the time he came to her, she had the feeling that she was trapped by this inevitable verse and had to "take her medicine." Being a devout woman, she no doubt would have welcomed such a reading under different circumstances and with more personal meaning and appropriateness. This is an extreme case; but it illustrates the danger of the pastor's getting into a rut.

Unfortunately, prayer can also become a stereotyped routine, through which a minister passes because he thinks it is expected, or a way out of a long call, which he should have terminated half an hour ago but now desperately concludes by saying, "Let us pray." Prayer should rather be a natural part of the pastoral call, used when it seems it would be well received and used in such a way as to include all the needs and concerns expressed by the patient during the call. Then, also, the prayer is more likely to become the patient's prayer, not just an embarrassing interlude. The attitude of naturalness and faith which the pastor expresses during prayer will carry over to and influence the patient's receptivity and willingness for prayer.

When a patient is very ill or semiconscious, familiar prayers and Scripture passages should be used because they can be more easily followed by a person in a weakened condition. One should always assume that the patient can hear what is being said and not whisper in the room of a comatose or dying person. The sense of hearing is said to be one of the last to leave the person. A benediction can be especially meaningful in such instances.

Holy Communion is especially appreciated when a patient requests it or has responded positively to a casual invitation. The main thing to bear in mind is that it should be the patient's genuine desire that dictates its administration, and not just the minister's notion that the patient should have it or perhaps a wife's request. In churches where adequate preparation is strongly recommended before receiving the sacrament, it would be possible to create added guilt feelings by urging Communion upon a patient prematurely. Most people know that this is available to them merely for the asking. In fact, it would be a good general rule to follow that the expressed needs of the patient are the best guide to the appropriateness of any of the various pastoral resources at any given time.

BEING CONCERNED — THE ACID TEST

No matter how smoothly the minister moves from one resource to another or uses "techniques" of counseling, if he does not basically feel a genuine and emotional concern for the patient, all his efforts will be minimized as professional sham. What one fine physician said about the spirit of his profession could also be applied as one of the criteria of good pastoral care of the sick, in fact, the acid test. "One of the essential qualities of the clinician is interest in humanity, for the secret of the care of the sick is in caring for the patient" (*Ibid.*, p. 48).

Paul Johnson stresses this same characteristic as the core of the chaplain's function: "The hospital patient needs a chaplain to bridge the social distance to his island of pain by representing someone who cares and heals," ("Psychological Aspects of the Chaplain's Work," *Bulletin of the American Protestant Hospital Association,* Vol. XIV, May, No. 3, 1950). The pastor believes that at the very center of the universe there is a loving God who cares for each person, and he is motivated by this same divine love as manifested through Jesus Christ, the Great Physician. Being thus concerned for people in need, the one seeking to bring pastoral care to the sick is more likely to use these wonderful and powerful resources more effectively.

It would be possible to list an impressive catalogue of specific "Do's and Don't's" in making a pastoral call, such as: Don't sit on or jiggle the bed. Don't stay too long. Don't ask embarrassing questions about the patient's illness. Don't pry into the person's life and background. Don't give medical advice, etc. But more important and helpful in learning pastoral care is the continual practice of putting oneself in the patient's place, trying to understand his condition and situation, and caring for a fellow human being in need. As such concern and empathy develop, inappropriate and harmful practices are less likely to intrude into the pastoral call. Being concerned is more a matter of attitude than of carefully applied techniques. The patient quickly senses whether the pastoral call is a forced and contrived duty or a natural and spontaneous expression of concern on the part of one of God's ministers.

◁ 5 ▷

LEARNING FROM CLINICAL EXPERIENCE

LEARNING by doing is a vital phase of modern education; yet one does not always learn constructively from his experience. A person's bad habits and hostile attitudes can become as firmly entrenched through repetition as can creative ones. Thus, the mere fact that a pastor has had ten years' experience in ministering to the sick does not necessarily mean that he has increased in effectiveness year by year. What must he do with this experience in order to learn creatively from it? The necessary self-analysis is possible when one has objectively recorded his evaluation and then has tried to view it with detached honesty. Such honesty is essential in pastoral care because self-deception and rationalization destroy the pastoral relationship. If the pastor hopes to help the parishioner or patient accept himself honestly, he must be willing to evaluate his own pastoral work with the same candor.

Making a record of the pastoral call forces the student to analyze his motivation, methods, attitudes, and sensitivity to another's needs and feelings. As soon as the student has made the call, he should record it while the experience is still fresh and vital in his memory. He should go immediately to the nearest place of privacy where he can jot down his impressions, the verbatim account of the conversation, emotional overtone, and his own feelings about the pastoral relationship. He must try to abandon himself to recording everything that took place without asking himself if it were successful, justifiable, or " good counseling"; later he can ask these questions. The immediate task is to reproduce as completely and objectively as possible (like a physicist reporting honestly the weights and measures of his work) the actual facts and events of his pastoral call in proper sequence.

The next day, or after his instructor has returned the " Record of Pastoral Call " with critical comments, the student reads the same words and views the same events from a new perspective. He is surprised to discover how often he had abruptly changed the conversation, how judgmental he actually had been, how many other Scripture passages would have been more appropriate, or how his prayer had not included the person's real problem or his expressed need. Could it be that the call was less patient-centered than he had hoped and more pastor-centered than he had imagined? Now he sees all these mistakes on paper, which he would have passed by unnoticed if he had not forcibly confronted himself with the objective facts in black and white. He can gain all this by recording his experience in the clinical setting.

Because most of us become defensively involved in rationalization and self-justification, it is helpful to have another person view our work more objectively and point out significant interpretations that we have been unable to make for ourselves. Students of social work recognize the need of a supervisor's evaluating their case histories and recorded interviews. Just as the counselee needs an understanding and accepting person with whom to share his growth, so the student needs a skillful, understanding colleague with whom to share new insights and self-criticism. This is a golden opportunity for personal development as well as professional growth in pastoral care.

In clinical pastoral education it is of inestimable value to have a supervisor, hospital chaplain, or instructor who is acquainted with the situation in which the student is working make pertinent comments on the record of the call. Therefore, on the suggested outline for " Record of Pastoral Call " (see page 79 for a typical form used with variations in many centers) there should be a three-inch margin on the right side of the sheet for the supervisor's comments. Ideally, the student should confer with the supervisor frequently to discuss these comments and the pastoral calling in general. During this discussion many factors may emerge which were omitted from the written account.

Explanation of the "Record of Pastoral Call"

The *student* should always identify himself by name. Also give the *course* or other auspices under which the call was made. The *date* is necessary to identify the call in relation to time of admission, surgery, and treatments, as well as other calls made on the same patient.

Identification of the patient upon whom the call was made should conform to the practice of the hospital and the supervisor. Use initials to designate the hospital. Hospitals are necessarily careful that confidential information from a patient's case record will not fall into the wrong hands. It is sufficient to identify patients by Roman numerals and indicate the number of the particular call by Arabic numbers. This is a simple *code number*. Thus the student's first call on his first patient would be I, 1. In the case of the fourth recorded call on the third patient in the student's series, the number would be III, 4. Take every precaution not to lose or mislay the "Record of Pastoral Call." Also guard against careless talk in wards,

RECORD OF PASTORAL CALL

Student_____   Code   No._____

Course_____   Date of Call_____

Supervisor_____   Type_____

I. *Preliminary Information*

State the source of referral and all facts you know about the patient, his background, diagnosis, and need.

(Leave three-inch margin for supervisor's comments.)

II. *Preparation*

Why are you making this call? How does the factual information influence your attitude, plans, and preparation?

(Do not include here anything you learned from the call itself.)

III. *Observations*

What sights, sounds, or smells impress you upon entering the room? Note the physical and social setting, the demeanor and appearance of the patient.

IV. *Interpersonal Relationship*

What was said and done by each of you, the feeling tone as well as the objective conversation? Trace the actual sequence as far as possible in a verbatim record. Separate nonverbal communication by parentheses. Double-space between quotations.

(Save all interpretations for the "Evaluation.")

(Number your conversations using C1, C2, etc., for chaplain's statements and P1, P2, etc., for patient's statements.)

V. *Evaluation*

1. *Summary and analysis* of what happened. List insights gained into the patient's situation, feelings, implications of your call. Be objective.

2. *Self-criticism.* What mistakes did you make, and how were you successful?

(Perhaps you gained insight into yourself.)

3. *Opportunities* for future calls, referrals to other resources (professional, social, spiritual, etc.). How far along has this person come in spiritual growth and maturity?

(Try to relate your planning to the patient's capacities.)

4. *Time* and length of this call in minutes. Was the length appropriate? Did you have any difficulty in terminating the call?

corridors, or dormitories, and family circles, because you do not know who might be the patient's neighbor, business acquaintance, relative, or friend. Nothing could damage your pastoral relationship or hinder the chaplaincy program in the hospital more than carelessness in this regard. Be sure to mention intervening visits made between recorded calls under the section entitled "Preliminary Information."

Use the space for *type* of call only if it is helpful. Perhaps a student notices that he has difficulty with certain types of calls, such as introductory calls, calls on the aged, the dying, children, or women. It might be useful to write up a series of such calls to learn why they are especially difficult for him. This method of learning pastoral care by recording calls can be adapted and modified to suit the needs of the student. However — and this is important — if using this term "type" makes the student feel that he is dealing with a "case" instead of a person, he had better not use it. Do not allow this process of recording and studying to mislead you into thinking of a fellow human being as just another "T.B. case," You are calling upon a *person,* who, amidst all his other experiences, feelings, and interpersonal relationships, is also now suffering from the disease of tuberculosis. You are not calling upon a "surgical case" but upon a *person,* who is undergoing the experience of surgery. Being objective in your recording and analysis of many calls should help you realize the unique individuality of each person and his situation.

Bearing in mind the above caution, it might still be useful to sum up the call under a "type." Then, as the collection of calls is studied in the class, there may be generalizations to be made about differences between calling on the aged as compared with calling on the adolescent or the middle-aged. Are there general similarities among chronic, contagious, and "bone and joint" patients? The obvious differences are suggested by the fact that the hospital groups patients by diseases or treatment in a variety of ways (e.g., surgical, medical, and obstetric wards). Use any classification that will be meaningful and instructive.

Leave a blank for the *supervisor's* name because it is an essential part of the learning process to share the insights and criticisms of another person who can view our work objectively and point out issues and opportunities that we have missed. No student should be surprised if he occasionally becomes irritated and even angry because of criticisms. That is merely an accurate sign that a sore spot has been touched, which it will very likely be most productive to pursue further. Remember our plea for frankness, objectivity, and a willingness to grow personally.

I. Preliminary Information

Facts known in advance can often give the pastoral caller valuable clues to the patient's condition. The carbon copy of the admission slip, which is sometimes sent routinely to the chaplain's office, may include the following information:

Name Doe, John Albert		Case No. 354082	Class 11A	Room number 213 W	
Address 216 Oak Street, Athens, Ohio		Marital Status Single		Sex M	Age 16
Date of Birth 2/10/39	Birthplace Chicago, Ill.	Occupation Mechanic	Color W	Religion Prot.	
Nearest Relative Andrew U. Brown		Address 216 Oak Street, Athens, Ohio		How Related Grandfather	
Date of Admission 4/10/55		Time 10:45 P.M.		Provisional Diagnosis Appendicitis	
Hospital Insurance Blue Cross		Previous Admission 10/5/49		Physician Dr. N.Q. Jones	

Note unusual combinations such as a maternal grandfather listed as the nearest of kin even though the boy is only sixteen years old. An apparently full-time occupation is indicated; perhaps he has dropped out of school at the minimum legal age. His being admitted at 10:45 P.M. suggests an emergency. The term "Provisional Diagnosis" refers to the first impression of the admitting doctor, but it may be modified after further observation and tests. Although you should be careful not to form rigidly preconceived notions about the boy, you can enter his hospital room much more alert for various stresses that might be inherent in his life situation.

Include under this preliminary information anything the nurse, doctor, or chaplain-supervisor has told you about the patient. It is helpful to know if he has had recent treatment, surgery, or a "hypo" to make him sleep. Often certain advance information will change your plans and goals so that you can minister more effectively by postponing your visit or by acting differently in some way. In later reports include all you have learned about the patient under this heading because it has a bearing upon the present call. By stating the source of referral, you indicate who is concerned enough about the patient to ask you to see him — nurse, psychiatrist, social worker, relative, or chaplain; or the name may simply have appeared on a routine list of new admissions.

II. PREPARATION

In the light of your preliminary information, how can your call be most useful for this person? After considering your reasons for calling on the sick in the hospital, focus your attention and interest on this patient in particular. Note your own attitude and mood, whether or not you "feel like making a call today." Perhaps in a corridor for a brief moment you prayed for guidance and a helpful, understanding approach to this person in need. If there have been previous calls on this patient, you will benefit by reviewing them in your mind or checking written reports on them. Sometimes you have come away from other calls with definite self-criticisms which you will want to concentrate on eliminating this time. Such thoughtful preparation equips you to enter upon any call with more confidence. Surely our ministry is worthy of the same careful preparation and forethought used by other professionals on the health team working with the same patient.

III. OBSERVATIONS

Unless you are able to take in the scene at a glance, you will miss many clues to understanding the patient and his situation. What seems to be the relationship with other persons in the room? Pretend that you are a camera making a photographic recording of the patient in his setting. If you have really been "exposed" to him, you should be able to report enough details so that the supervisor reading your report can visualize the sun-tanned face, the working-man's hands, the furrowed brow, the prematurely gray hair, the engagement ring, the luxurious bathrobe on the chair, the look of worry and fatigue as distinct from sharp pain, or whatever else may impress you upon entering the patient's room. The total picture is made up of hundreds of details: smells, sights, noises, the physical and social setting. Note the rumpled bed clothing and mussed hair or the neat appearance of the person and room. Are there no greeting cards even on February 14 or in the Easter season? You cannot know what all these details mean in the patient's total experience, but these observations will take on meaning as your call progresses. Keen observation helps you stay alert; and the patient senses that you care.

IV. Interpersonal Relationship

This is the call itself. By making a verbatim record of your pastoral call you are forced to concentrate and listen to another person's statements and questions more closely than you have ever done before in your life. In the same way that exercise in observation helps you see more clearly, trying to record conversation makes you a better listener. Our pastoral calls are often ineffective because we are only half alert to what our parishioners are saying and too intent on our own wandering thoughts, problems, and projects; thus we miss valuable leads and are disappointed that persons do not share their real concerns with us. The sad truth may be that while someone has tried to share and open up his life to us, we have been too preoccupied with other things to notice or accept his invitation. Do not be disappointed if remembering and recording your interview is difficult at first; you will improve with practice and be well repaid for your efforts.

By numbering your statements, you can more easily refer to them in the "Evaluation" section of the report. Thus, C1 (C stands for chaplain or student) is the first statement you make upon entering the room, and P1 is the first statement the patient makes. Double-space between speeches to make the dialogue stand out. Clearly indicate responses made by other persons in the room, such as visitors or roommates. There is no need for quotation marks because it is assumed that all material is as nearly verbatim as you can make it. Nonverbal communications and events can be put in parentheses as follows:

(At this point the nurse brought his dinner tray.)

or

(The patient had been trying to hold back tears for some time but finally began to cry and wipe her eyes.)

or

(Roommate leaves the room.)

Save interpretations of these events and communications, as well as your reactions to them, for the "Evaluation" section. Keep this interview section as objective and detailed as possible. Catch the feeling tone as well as the factual content of the conversation on the part of both yourself and the patient.

V. EVALUATION

Do not try to cut corners in your evaluation because this is your opportunity to learn. Without evaluation you might have served as an excellent camera, microphone, and stenographer, but have failed in that acid test of scientific, professional competence: seeing meaningful relationships and significance in the vast assortment of data you have gathered. You squeeze your record like a sponge and dissect the interpersonal relationship like a biologist painstakingly trying to learn as much as possible from this experience. In proportion to your belief that yours is a high and holy calling, you will desire to evaluate carefully and honestly this function of making a pastoral call on a person in need.

1. *Summary and analysis.* First, summarize briefly all the topics that were discussed. Analyze your relationship: how you were received, how the call progressed, the influence of various events and persons in the room or ward, the influence of the patient's physical or mental condition on the conversation, attitudes of the patient toward the topics discussed. List insights you gained into the patient's family relationships, his vocational life, his way of looking at the world, his fears, hopes, faith, and countless other feelings and ideas and experiences he has shared with you.

Did this old grandmother look upon you as her son or grandson? Did the fact that you represent God and the Church encourage a hearty welcome or erect a barrier of hostility? Are you aware of any spiritual implications or growth as a result of this visit? Perhaps the patient was able to think, for the first time, of God as a loving Father, and thus dared to confess his sins and faults in a new confidence that he could be forgiven. He may have made progress in accepting himself realistically for the first time, acknowledging his limitations of personal capacity and social position. He might have received new strength to face a difficult necessity or fact, such as an amputation, the death of his mother or child, or even his own impending death. But, perhaps, instead of growing in grace, he has developed negatively, indicated that he is becoming more egocentric and self-pitying, more bitter and unbelieving, than before. In all this you are not to sit in divine judgment but humbly try to understand what has actually happened during your pastoral call in order that in the future you can serve this patient and others more effectively.

2. *Self-criticism* is a painful process because it is a threat to the beloved ego, our most prized possession. Yet it is absolutely necessary for maximum growth both personally and professionally. Our first tendency will be to hunt hard for valid reasons (more often excuses) for everything we did, justifying our actions and words and defending our integrity. A common and subtle temptation is to say something like this: "I realize that as a general rule one would not take this approach, *but* in this case I felt justified." Become suspicious of yourself if you find you are frequently pleading the special case and exception to the rule while the supervisor and other members of the class consistently feel your approach is not helpful. " Know thyself " is the best cure for nonconstructive use of our defense mechanisms.

Self-criticism is difficult in this field of pastoral counseling and pastoral care where it seems to be impossible to follow a simple formula or measure spiritual growth by a yardstick. No two patients are the same, nor are any two pastors identical; and — what complicates matters even more — both pastor and patient are not the same persons on Friday that they were on Monday. Therefore, there can be no attempt to pour every student into a standard mold; each must learn to become the best pastor he can and render a ministry within the limits of his own capacity. God uses each of us in a different way, knowing that some are vessels of gold and others of clay. Self-criticism is a humbling spiritual exercise in learning to know ourselves better and evaluate our work honestly.

3. *Opportunities* seen from this call can form a good foundation for the preparation of your next call on this same patient. Remembering that this is only a tentative "diagnosis," what do you feel are the real needs or problems of this patient; and how could the resources of pastoral care be of help to him? Perhaps he is about to be discharged and you feel it would be a service to refer his name to a local pastor near his home, so that he can be related to a church home. Perhaps the patient has brought up many questions which the county welfare worker could answer and follow through on. Opportunities for interprofessional co-operation and referral often multiply our effectiveness as we share the responsibility for the care of the patient. You may recognize the need to confer with the social worker, the doctor, or the nurse about the patient's condition or resources. Many kinds of opportunities may have grown out of your call, such as requests for Holy Communion by the clergyman of a certain denomination, devotional literature, etc. Keep asking yourself: Is everything being done that can be done? Naturally, you will avoid making suggestions or referrals over the heads of other members of the health team. Stay out of the fields of nursing care, medications, and treatments, and the admissions or credit departments. Be aware of the proper channels of communications and respect other personnel's rights and privileges if you wish to be included on the health team.

4. *Time* may seem to be a small matter, yet many pastors have difficulty with this factor. There is an appropriate time to terminate a pastoral call so that the maximum benefit is achieved. It is possible to overstay one's welcome, to allow the conversation to go back over repetitious material in an endless circuitous pattern. It is easy to overtax a weak patient's strength or to talk too long about an emotion-laden problem. Perhaps your particular problem is to know how and when to terminate the call. It is easy to fall into a rut, a routine method of "getting out" of a room; just as a pastoral caller can develop a stereotyped method of introduction and initiating the call. Record the time of the call in minutes, and comment on why you left when you did.

There is value in going over this entire "Record of Pastoral Call" with the chaplain-supervisor or other instructor after he has made his comments in the wide right-hand margin, to be sure that you both have the same things in mind and are speaking the same language. He may need to have some of your statements clarified and enlarged upon. You may feel that much of the tone of the call was lost in transcribing and want to describe the situation in more detail, having remembered items now that you failed to include earlier.

WHAT WOULD YOU HAVE SAID AND DONE?

The following pastoral calls were made by students under the supervision of the author and are illustrative of how to write up such calls. They are not offered as ideal standards but as an approach that has been found useful for learning pastoral care over a period of years in many centers. There is room for much honest difference of opinion, and it is hoped that these calls will stimulate thought and discussion. All names of persons and places are fictitious or concealed.

A. Old, Sick, and Alone

RECORD OF PASTORAL CALL

Student	*John Jones*
Course	*Pastoral Counseling Seminary*
Supervisor	*Professor Belgum*
Code No.	I, 3, U.H.
Date of Call	*October 13, 195–*
Type	*Chronic Arthritic and Aged*

I. *Preliminary Information*

Mrs. M. is seventy-six years old, the recent (Sept. 12) widow of a Protestant minister, to whom she had been married for fifty-five

years. Most of their life together had been spent in a large upstate city where she worked with children in the church school. There is one son (married, with two children); a daughter died some years ago. M. and her son seem to be very close.

When was patient admitted?

This is the correct use of the known facts when you have had previous contacts with the patient. It helps you to integrate previous insights and information with the present call.

A previous interview indicated a rather deep sense of grief at the death of her husband; she spoke of him with difficulty. She has been cheerful and friendly on all other visits; her interests seem to center around her own work with children. She has spoken often of faith, stressing its importance to healthful living, implying, but not stating, a possible doubt concerning the reality of her own expressed faith.

She may need to talk about her husband, especially if she has not done the necessary grief work.

She may interpret her sickness as indication of lack of faith.

M. has attended the chapel services at the hospital and has expressed gratitude for them and for their meaning to her. In the two previous visits, there was no reticence on her part; she has been willing to talk freely. However, much of her conversation has remained on a relatively superficial level, with several definite indications that she was avoiding any movement into the areas of possible deep concern — for example, her husband's death, and her own attitude of faith.

This strengthens your pastoral relationship; services of worship and pastoral calls should supplement each other.

She may not yet have decided she wants to share these things with you, or she has come to an acceptance of these concerns that is satisfactory to her.

She has a definite, clear religious orientation, making daily use of the Bible and other devotional material.

It is good for you to realize total religious life as the context into which your call on this patient fits.

II. *Preparation*

Before entering the ward, I reviewed the notes from the previous visits. I recognize that my own interpretation of M.'s behavior might well cause me to attempt to direct the conversation into those areas which seem *to me* most important; part of my preparation was to redetermine to keep the locus of attention with M. as much as possible. My preparatory prayer was for the personal willingness to be interested in her concerns, and for the sensitivity to recognize and understand the motive forces within her.

Helpful for refreshing your memory and to see what direction the calls have gone, whether in a continuous direction or in pendulum fashion.

You are right about the locus of attention; it is still the patient's call and her concerns should guide you.

This is a constructive beginning of your call.

III. *Observations*

All three patients were in the ward when I entered. The two younger women were talking and smoking. M. was in her bed, lying flat with her chin in a weighted " harness " to maintain tension on the upper spine. There were flowers and cards on the table, along with the Bible and other pieces of literature. M. was dressed neatly, with a satin bed jacket on; her hair was combed. As I entered, I spoke to all the patients; observing M.'s position, I almost changed my mind and went to the bedside of one of the others, but M. asked me to sit down, saying that she would be " out of harness " in a few minutes. She seemed quite glad to see me.

Your alert observation helps orient you to her social setting, her mood, range of movement, etc., and helps establish good rapport even before the verbal part of the call begins.

Often this nonverbal communication and taking stock of each other are a significant part of the call.

Observations cover what you absorb of the situation before the conversation begins.

What of her size, countenance, personal appearance, etc.

IV. *Interpersonal Relationship*

P1. Please sit down. I'll be able to take this harness off in about ten minutes. I wear it for an hour at a time.

Her initiative is a good omen and indicates an adequate relationship from previous calls.

C1. It doesn't look like the most comfortable way to spend an hour.

You follow her lead carefully.

P2. It's uncomfortable all right, but if it will help me feel better, I'll do just about anything. They have a lot of things around here to help us. I don't like a lot of them, but I'm willing to do anything that will help me get well.

(She went on to describe at some length the various " tricks and gadgets " the hospital used. It was evident that she felt better than in the previous weeks, and that she credited much to the " gadgets." Her sense of humor was good; she could joke about feeling like " an old gray mare harnessed in her stall." After a few minutes, she looked at her watch and said: " Well, I guess I've had this thing on long enough. I'll take it off now so we can look at each other while we talk." Eye contact during this and other visits was almost constant. She unbuckled her harness with some difficulty and sat up.)

Although verbatim material is better, such a summary is better than leaving a gap in the call.

C2. Feels good to get out of it, doesn't it?

Don't use rhetorical questions as a general rule.

P3. It sure does, but it's worth it.

I'm going to be able to go home in a week or so.

C3. You've shown a lot of progress then.

Patients may go home because they have improved or their case is hopeless.

P4. Oh, I feel a lot better. The doctor told me yesterday that he thought I would be ready to go home pretty soon. I'll be glad to get out of here too; it's a pretty expensive place, especially for a minister's wife. But I don't mind paying for treatment that does me this much good.

(Pause. We had talked before of the expense involved; I didn't feel that she was vitally interested in talking about money, so I waited to let her take up the conversation.)

You are wise in letting her choose the area of interest.

Say, have you had any contact with *Unity?*

(On a previous visit, we had discussed some of this literature; she had shown some opposition to the movement, so I felt that here was an opportunity to move into an area of relatively strong feeling.)

C4. I've seen some of their literature. You don't accept much of what they say, do you?

O.K. — an open-ended reply — Rather, " I remember we discussed *Unity* before." Then she can pick it up again.

P5. Oh, it's wonderful!! I read an article this week that told how so much of our trouble is just in our minds. It's faith that counts. Could I read you a poem my brother sent me? It shows how important faith really is.

Quote this reference to family relationship.

(How wrong can one be? Here is a good example of how feeling may *not* carry over from one interview to another.)

Save comment for "evaluation," but a good observation. People are often ambivalent in attitudes and vacillate on the same topic.

C5. Faith has meant an awful lot to you.

Your hypothesis was she does not have so much faith as she said; have you changed your opinion?

P6. Oh, it has. Here, listen to this.

(She took a letter from the table and read the poem, a beautiful thing expressing faith and dependence on God.)

Isn't that true? We can do so much more if we will just leave things in God's hands.

C6. So often, we try to do things ourselves and almost forget God.

Responsive, shows you understand what she's trying to say.

P7. Faith is the way people get well. That's why it's so important to teach little children to believe in God. When I was teaching children, I *really* taught them. All this coloring they do now is a waste of time. I never read to them. I studied the lesson and then taught it to them in Sunday school. I used flannelgraph pictures with children and adults. They like the pictures and they learn so much from them.

(Here is an example of how a change in the conversation is made just when we seem to be beginning to explore an area of real importance to the patient.)

Put this in the "evaluation"; it is not part of the verbatim account. Would it have been useful to return to the subject of the difficulty of having enough faith in God? Patient may resent "exploring" or probing some areas.

C7. You've found pictures a really effective way of teaching them.

P8. We remember ten times as much of what we see as what we hear. And we remember more of what happened when we were young than what happens more recently. My grandmother was eighty-one when she died; she was paralyzed for a long time. She could remember a lot of things she did as a young girl, but the things that happened just a week ago — she just couldn't remember them.

It is helpful to let her dwell on what have been satisfying experiences to her, such as teaching.
Note identification with her grandmother and compare ages.

C8. The things that happen to us when we're young stay with us longer.

Effective use of "we" and "us" without straining to identify.

P9. That's just why it's so important to teach children the truths about life. Those things stay with them. Just last night, a woman visited me whom I had taught in Sunday school when she was a little girl. And once in the Trinity Church in Midville a woman came up to me and said: "You are Mrs. M. aren't you? Do you remember me? You were my Sunday school teacher when I was a little girl." When I get home, I want to teach in the _____ Church, if there is a children's class. I won't join the church, but I'll attend and I'll work in the Sunday school. We've got to teach the children the truths about God and Christ.

C9. They think a lot more than we give them credit for.

The significant part of her preceding statement, P8, was that her work was remembered; you could have responded to this in C9.

P10. They feel things too. And it's so satisfying to see them grow and to be good men and women, when they've had good training.

(Long pause.)

You maybe discovered it was just as useful to wait out the pause as to try to fill it in with words.

By the way, are you interested in leprosy work?

C10. I know a lot of wonderful work has been done in leper colonies. You evidently have a special interest in that work — is that right?

Your hunch that she wants to tell you all about it is correct.

P11. Missionaries are doing a great work in leper colonies.

(She went on to describe in detail the visit of a missionary to the church her husband served. She told of a movie shown by this man, and of his stay in the parsonage.)

I still contribute regularly as much as I can. I just recently sent him a check and got a personal letter back from him. He told me he wanted to do more than just send the regular " thank you " letter. And he remembered the time he had been in our house so many years ago. It's wonderful what our missionaries are doing. And we should be training more children to give their lives to missionary work. There isn't anything so satisfying as to see a child grow up and dedicate his whole life to Christ and Christian work. Does your wife teach in Sunday school?

Remembering that her husband died only a month ago, note her references to home and indirectly to him. These are leads and hints.

C11. She has taught, but she isn't teaching right now. I don't know if she'll have a record of fifty-five years' work in the church or not.

You're correct; she didn't really want to talk about your wife; you turn it back quietly.

P12. It's been wonderful. We've made so many friends. And they are still our friends. I think that is a pretty good recommendation.

Older people like and need reassurance, and often reassure themselves. Your response is helpful in this supportive way.

C12. The fact that they are still good friends of yours indicates that you've done a pretty good job of living.

P13. I think it's a good recommendation.

(Pause.)

I got a letter this week from a man; he told me he thought I ought to live in my own home instead of going to my son's home. His wife died five years ago and he stayed right in their home and it did him a lot of good. I wrote and told him I intend to stay in my home. I wouldn't want to be anywhere else.

She is getting back to one of her problems, which confronts many old people, especially when they are somewhat incapacitated.

C13. There is another family in part of your house, isn't there, so you won't be completely alone?

A positive note brought in from a previous call no doubt.

P14. Yes, and the woman is a trained nurse. And, besides, I have my two parakeets and they have been a real comfort to me. They are called "comfort birds" and they really are.

C14. They live up to their name for you, then?

Responsive, you are trying to understand what this all means for her.

P15. Oh, yes. I talk to them all day. They are something alive in the house with me. When I get up in the morning, I take them into the kitchen with me. And if I'm in the dining room, writing or something, I have them right on the table with me. I suppose the people downstairs wonder who I talk to, but I think they understand. I want to stay in my own home so that I can be independent. My older sister is ill too, so I couldn't go to her. And my brother and his wife have three children of their own; that's enough for anyone to have to care for. If you're staying in someone else's house, no matter who it is, you feel obligated to think of them.

You afford her the opportunity to rethink out loud her reasons for deciding to live in her own home.

C15. You can't have the feeling of independence you want that way.

Responsive. Instead of telling her what to do you share her thinking.

P16. Of course, my brother will spend the first night with me. But, I can do my exercises there and everything the doctors have told me to do. And it will be less expensive for me to be home. I'll be glad to get out of the hospital.

C16. Will you be here when I come next week?

This shows your continuing interest and helps to prepare for the possibility that this may be the last time you'll see her.

P17. I probably shall. Do you have to leave now?

(I stood up as she spoke.)

Will you read something before you go?

C17. Is there something particular you would like to hear?

(She left the decision to me and I read from I John, ch. 4. We had prayer, and I prayed for a strengthening of our faith to meet all of life. The interview closed with her remark, " I hope I'll see you next week.")

You did well to fulfill her request and then leave, as it is your responsibility to structure the conclusion of the call as you must the beginning introduction. If you can remember the prayer, it is good to include it. What verses did you read and do you explain your choice under " Evaluation " ?

V. *Evaluation*

1. *Summary and analysis:* This interview, as the others with M., went smoothly, perhaps almost too smoothly to have touched on any really significant areas of thinking or feeling. Both of us enjoyed the conversation; M. felt free to talk, but she did seem to avoid any prolonged exploration of her own faith and she showed no desire to bring into the conversation her husband's death or her feelings about it. Reviewing the interview, I find no real continuity in thought, perhaps another indication that we dealt primarily with superficial matters. Her constant returning to her work with children seems to indicate something, but I do not know what it is. There has been a real improvement in her general attitude; she is more cheerful than on previous occasions. No doubt the fact that she is anticipating going home has a lot to do with this.

There has been an interesting correlation between M.'s arthritic condition and her husband's health;

These have been largely supportive calls to help her over stressful situations, such as her husband's death and her hospitalization and return home. It is doubtful if she needs any basic reorientation or change of attitude at this stage of life. She has a pretty stable attitude for her age.

If you were going to follow up her topics related to her husband, it should be done at the time of such remarks: but once she has gone on to teaching, etc., it is best not to bring the subject up out of context. Appropriate times to have discussed such topics would have been after P4, " expensive . . . for a minister's wife "; P11, missionary who stayed in the parsonage; or P13, " stay in my home."

last spring, when he had to give up his work, she suffered quite a bit, and within the month following his death she was in the hospital. This of course says nothing definite about the relationship between her emotional and physical states, but it would be interesting to be able to follow through and see if any real correlation could be established. However, chances are that this will be our last interview. (This was the case. The following week she was preparing to leave with her son. Our relationship was ended then on a mutually friendly basis.)

2. *Self-criticism:* I believe that I was able to stay with M. during this interview better than other times. At least, there were fewer obvious mistakes in reflecting feeling. There was a strong tendency on my part to try to lead our thinking into those areas I felt were important, but I feel that we did follow M.'s line of thought; it may be, however, that my desires, though not expressed, were communicated to M., with the result that when we began to explore those "tender" areas she defended herself by changing the line of conversation. Although outwardly the interview was "client-centered," I'm not sure that it was in reality. I find too that at times I get too wrapped up in mechanics — trying to be sure I'll remember a particular response or feeling — to re-

Correct — there often is a correlation between emotional stresses and the intensity of arthritic symptoms. If she had stayed another month, you might have become more involved about the husband. Perhaps she felt more professionally competent than he — note references to her teaching skill and important missionary work, but no mention of her husband's accomplishments. You help to prepare her for the termination of your relationship.

This was an excellent call. It may have been a bit long, but perhaps you could judge that she did not seem overtired.

As far as one can sense from the recorded call, this is a helpful and responsive relationship, and pastoral in the best sense. It is often difficult to be pastoral with a member of a pastor's family as the role has mixed meanings to them.

spond really adequately to what is being expressed.

3. *Opportunities:* There will probably be little opportunity for any further work with M., but I believe that it is evident that with proper understanding and acceptance it would be possible for her to explore her own self quite deeply, and enable her to cope more realistically with her life situation.

It seems she has a pretty realistic adjustment to her situation within the scope of her capacity, although the possibility of psychosomatic implications is reasonable. Remember that major personality reorientation at her age is difficult.

4. *Time:* 11:08–11:45 A.M., approximately 37 minutes. At least an additional 30 minutes were spent immediately following this call in preparing the notes in order to make as full a report as possible.

This patient remarked to me at chapel service how much she had appreciated your calls.

B. Four Calls on a Surgical Patient

RECORD OF PASTORAL CALL

Student _____ *Seminarian Jones*

Course _____ *Pastoral Counseling, Sem.*

Supervisor _____ *Professor Belgum*

Code No. _____ I, 1, C.H.

Date of Call _____ *Feb. 26, 195–*

Type _____ *Surgical*

I. *Preliminary Information*

Patient was on the surgical floor, having been admitted less than a week ago. He had been referred to me by the chaplain-supervisor from the list of new admissions.

You don't have much to go on here, but it might be an advantage sometimes not to be prejudiced by preconceived notions.

II. *Preparation*

I wish to establish an acquaintance with this man — to discover all I can about him — so as to establish rapport.

Be careful not to plan to probe or dig for facts. Achieve rapport by showing empathy and understanding.

III. *Observations*

Upon entering the room, I noticed that P. was lying in bed with his legs up. Both legs were bandaged completely. P. was reading from a coil-bound book which looked like a manual of some sort. He had the looks of a laborer — rough hands and leathery complexion. He wore glasses — behind which were what looked like awfully tired eyes. His hair, though thinning considerably, was not yet gray. P. had absolutely no flowers in the room and no cards were in sight. He had no wedding ring on. The room was a wreck — ash trays and cigarette stubs littered the place. The dresser scarf was rumpled and the furniture was haphazardly placed.

Excellent description. I can picture this man and his room because you were observant.

IV. *Interpersonal Relationship*

C1. Hello, there. I'm Bill Jones from the seminary. Heard you were here and thought I'd drop up to see how you were getting along.

The nurse is called Miss Jones, and the physician Dr. Jones. You suggested a buddy-buddy relationship by your introduction.

P1. Smith's my name. Glad to see you.

Leave out patient's real name. An initial would be safer.

C2. Things moving along O.K. for you?

Hoping for the optimistic answer perhaps.

P2. Yep. Had a touch of gangrene in my feet, but the Doc's got it licked now.

(I thought contact was coming to an end here.)

Do you mean that if he does not have a " problem " you can leave? Don't jump to conclusions or take everything patient says at face value.

C3. When did you come out here?

Fact-finding not nearly so useful as responding to his statement in P2.

P3. Couple days ago. None too soon either. Called the doctor and was out here inside of fifteen minutes.

Looks like the gangrene really was important, hardly just " a touch."

C4. Gangrene can be nasty stuff.

(He then opened up for the first time and began talking about it.)

That's better, but why generalize?

P4. I had diabetes for twenty-five years, and phlebitis for twenty years. That's what caused my gangrene. When you get phlebitis, your legs swell up. My shoe wore a blister on my ankle. It broke and gangrene set in.

C5. You can't fool around with it, can you?

Responsive to his remark about hurrying to the hospital, P3.

P5. Nope. I had a specialist I knew twenty years ago. He really knew his stuff. When all the other doctors only aggravated my condition, he came in and cured me.

C6. It sure helps a lot to have confidence in your doctor.

Will he have the same confidence today he had twenty years ago?

P6. Yep. The one I have now is a peach. Wouldn't be here today if it weren't for him. He operated a year ago for ulcers — took biggest part of my stomach out.

Ulcers are often caused by or aggravated by anxiety and emotional stress. Compare with P8 and P10 — exacting work.

(Pause.)

(Patient picks up book he had been reading when I entered.)

P7. Just looking over some of the diesel engines. Got to keep up on them so I can keep ahead of the boys.

C7. Do you work at M _____ Co.?

Don't get ahead of him. Rather, "You work with diesels and find it pretty exacting."

P8. No. I'm maintenance supervisor for the railroad. Improvements being made all the time. Gotta keep up with them.

C8. I used to work on diesels. We had two of them for our main engines on my ship in the Navy.

Such identification you no doubt intended to foster rapport but can sidetrack conversation onto yourself and away from patient.

P9. Yeah, they use the same thing there. Here's a picture of it. Look familiar?

C9. It sure does. They're interesting things.

P10. Can't beat them; kinda tricky, though, if you don't know your stuff.

(Then he related a couple of experiences when engines broke down en route. Engineers had to call him to locate the trouble. He figured out the trouble and told

Notice he's more interested in relating *his* experiences than in hearing about your Navy experiences.

them over the phone what to do. Fixing engines without even seeing them!)

I just try to pass on what I know to others in my little way.

C10. There's a lot of satisfaction in being able to do that.

This is your value judgment; evidently you sensed it was his also.

P11. My boys do O.K. once I get them trained. I don't have much to worry about. Hope to get back to them before too long, though.

C11. You say the doctor has your gangrene licked?

Why do you change the subject here instead of responding to his attitude toward being off the job?

P12. Yeah, it won't be long now before I'll be back.

C12. That's good. Gotta run now. Glad to have seen you.

Better not to make value judgments very often such as, "that's good," or, "that's too bad"; rather remain more objective and simply show understanding of situation. Also, your comment, "Gotta run now," suggests you're in a hurry.

P13. Glad to talk with you too.

V. *Evaluation*

I thought I was going to lose this patient before we got started. He had told me what was wrong with him. It was with some difficulty that the conversation was kept moving. Finally we found common ground (diesel engines) and a friendly attitude and relationship developed.

I received the impression that this man was all wrapped up in his

It usually takes people a little time to open up to a perfect stranger, even if he claims to be a pastor, who is naturally interested. You missed the other problems he spoke of before the diesel topic came up.

work. He couldn't even leave it long enough to come to the hospital. He had had several close calls physically in his life. He was glad to have a doctor he could trust. He didn't seem particularly worried about anything. He had resigned himself to his diseases and was quite willing to make the necessary adjustments to live with them. He struck me as being another of those "self-made men," needing no help from anyone.

Time of this call: About twelve minutes.

Isn't it possible that unconsciously he might wonder whether this gangrene situation woud turn out to be another "close call"? Note in P3 how he was rushed to the hospital.

Strong, "self-made men" often have the greatest difficulties admitting their fears and worries, are afraid to lose face.

You have said nothing about self-criticism or future opportunities — both very important.

Series B. Continued

RECORD OF PASTORAL CALL

Student   *Seminarian Jones*

Course   *Pastoral Counseling, Sem.*

Supervisor   *Professor Belgum*

Code No.   I, 2, C.H.

Date of Call   *March 5, 195–*

Type   *Surgical*

I. *Preliminary Information*

Patient is hospitalized with gangrene as a result of burst blister on heel of left foot. P. works for the railroad as maintenance foreman. I'd say he is in his early forties, and deeply engrossed in his work. From previous call, P. seemed to

Good summary of pertinent facts. Do you recall his physical appearance from your last call?

be all alone in the world. The
nurse said he'd probably be in the
hospital for another week.

II. *Preparation*

There was no special preparation for this call. I was mildly
curious to see what kind of reception I should receive, since in my
previous call I was all but shut out
in the first few minutes. I wanted
to be especially alert for signs of
friends.

The fact that your need for acceptance was not fully met last
time seems to have left you a bit
insecure and threatened.

III. *Observations*

Upon entering the patient's
room, I noticed P. sitting in the
chair in the opposite corner of the
room with his feet in a pan of
water. He had his glasses on — under the right lens was a black eye.
Exactly in between his right eye
and his rapidly receding hairline
was a patch of gauze and tape that
had not been there before. P. was
clean-shaven, but his ruddy-com-
plexioned face had that drawn look
of utter despair. Having seen P.
only once before, I had the impulse
to back away from the room and
leave, for I thought the patients
in this room had changed and this
was not P. But just as I was about
to leave, P. raised his right hand to
me in recognition.

You're picking up more details
than you did before.

There was a rather heavy-set
woman in the chair beside him.
She had a pleasant countenance.
Her round face looked almost jolly.

I would judge her to be in her early forties. She looked completely relaxed, and folded her hands lazily in her lap.

How do you suppose her presence will affect your relationship with the patient?

The dresser top was full of cards, carefully opened so that they could stand up by themselves, and they were strategically placed on the dresser. There was a tone of tidiness about the room that was completely lacking at my first visit.

You are wise to notice both social and physical changes in the patient's environment. It can be either the cause or the result of a change in patient's mood.

IV. *Interpersonal Relationship*

P1. Come on in. How are you to-night?

C1. Fine. But the question is: How are you? (Said with a grin.)

An effective and friendly way of turning attention back to him without strain.

P2. Coming along pretty good right now. Meet my wife, Mrs. P.

Wife. How do you do.

C2. I'm glad to know you, Mrs. P. Are you baby-sitting tonight?

Don't make jokes at patient's expense. Sometimes the dependency of a patient is embarrassing enough and painfully like that of infancy — feeding, bathing, care, etc.

Wife. Yes — tonight and every night. It gets to be quite a tiring trip over here.

C3. It can be tiring.

P3. It won't be much longer now. Should be out within a week.

C4. You should. (Said as neither a statement nor a question.)

You do well in remaining a bit noncommital. Let him expand it if he wishes.

P4. Yes (pointing to his heel), it's turned brown; shows it's nearing the surface.

C5. I can see the brownish color.

P5. It's a nasty-looking thing. (Pulling foot clear up so I can get a good look. It was!)

Do such sights upset you? Comment on it in your evaluations if they do.

Wife. Then, to make matters worse, he fell out of bed the other night.

C6. You did?

P6. Yeah, those beds are so narrow. I went to raise up in bed and my elbow slipped off the bed. I tumbled out on my head.

C7. You didn't roll in your sleep, then?

Why bring up this possibility? Don't add worries to those the patient already has.

P7. Well, no, but I was groggy from those sleeping pills.

C8. I see.

Wife. Instead of telling people he ran into the door, he can say the floor ran into him.

(Everyone had a good laugh.)

C9. Well, I was up this way and wanted to see how you were. I'll be running along now. I'll look in and see if you're here next week. Nice to have met you, Mrs. P.

No doubt you are trying to be casual and informal here. It was good to assure him of your continued interest and future visit if he's here.

P8. Do that. And thanks for stopping by. It's good to know someone's thinking of you.

This is his interpretation of the call and its value for him.

V. *Evaluation*

1. *Summary and analysis:* I actually found out more by observation this time than by conversation. I was curious about his friends and family. I met his wife, and noted the many cards, indicating friends and contacts.

I couldn't quite figure out the wife. She looked pleasant enough, but her conversation made him uneasy. She went off on her trouble having to visit the hospital, etc. When P. tells of his improved condition, she comes back with a statement like, "Then, to make matters worse . . ." Not too understanding.

Notice, however, both you and she made jokes at his expense.

P.'s condition seemed much improved, except for the additional patch on his head. But perhaps he was covering up his real feelings. He indicated satisfaction with the healing of his sore.

I was tempted to draw him out on what he meant by his last statement, but since I had said my farewell, I thought it best to leave.

I believe he would not have elaborated on P7 with his wife present. Yes, usually make your departure as clear and well-structured as your introduction.

2. *Self-criticism:* I feel that in this call I failed to get the conversation beyond the small talk. Looking back over the conversation, I can see no leads that would have guided it otherwise.

This frequently happens when a third party is present. The third party is often not able to be objective or understanding.

I was successful in finding out about his friends and family mostly by just observing the evidence. But I failed to develop anything about his friends from the cards clue.

Perhaps he would have mentioned the cards if he had really wanted to talk about those who sent them.

3. *Opportunities:* Remembering the difficulty in establishing rapport the first time, I am now hopeful that a real relationship may develop. I was selfishly pleased with the parting comment of Mr. P., and shall definitely plan to see him again (hopefully when his wife is not around).

Were there other topics of conversation not reported? You must have missed something as this report hardly represents a seven-minute conversation.

Try jotting down some notes at least immediately after the call in a private place, and writing up the report as soon as possible.

4. *Time:* Seven minutes.

Series B. Continued

RECORD OF PASTORAL CALL

Student	*Seminarian Jones*
Course	*Pastoral Counseling, Sem.*
Supervisor	*Professor Belgum*
Code No.	I, 3, C.H.
Date of Call	*March 12, 195–*
Type	*Surgical*

I. *Preliminary Information*

P. has been hospitalized for over three weeks with a case of gangrene in the left heel, which resulted from a blister. He is about forty years of age, with a wife who seems to consider him more of a burden than a mate. He works for the railroad as a maintenance foreman.

Remember all his sicknesses. Her patience may have been tried over the years.

At the last call, P. was in exceptionally good spirits. He was scheduled to go to surgery to have his heel operated on. But at that time he thought he would be out of the hospital in a week. However, the nurse told me just before this visit that he was scheduled for surgery Saturday (tomorrow), for an amputation! This took me completely by surprise, and it was all I could do to go through with this call. It was with some difficulty that I made myself go to his room this time.

One reason for not getting too enthusiastic about a patient's report of good news is just such unexpected surprises as this. It is better to be a bit more neutral and objective, so as to be available for either ups or downs.

II. *Preparation*

When I first went by P.'s room, I noticed a rather young couple milling about, so I went on to some other calls before I made this one. These other calls, I'm afraid, weren't too successful, since my mind was constantly on P. and whether or not I could handle the situation. As I went down the hall to P.'s room, I offered a prayer for guidance in meeting this situation, and for a way of helping P. meet the coming day and the loss of his leg.

You were wise in trying to arrange to see this man alone so that if he wants to vent his real feelings, he can do so. It is good that you recognize how really upset this news made you. You have to accept your own feelings before you can help him accept his.

III. *Observations*

I raised my hand in greeting as I walked into the room. P. was sitting in a chair on the far side of the room, shaving equipment spread out before him and lather all over his face. The black eye

Will you encourage him to finish shaving before you begin visiting with him or will you start right in?

of last visit was disappearing and the bandage which had been over his eye was gone.

The room was in pretty good order (better than usual). There were mechanic's manuals lying on the table beside the bed. The window sill was loaded with flowers. (He had never had flowers on previous visits.) And the greeting cards had greatly increased in number.

Sudden and unexpected large quantities of cards and flowers sometimes upset a patient, who begins to suspect he's worse off than anyone has dared to tell him.

IV. *Interpersonal Relationship*

C1. Am I interrupting you? (Raising my hand in recognition.)

P1. No — not at all. Come on in. Join me in a shave?

C2. Don't believe so. (Smiling along with P.) Have you moved out of that chair since last Friday?

Again joking, this time with a man who may just spend a lot of time confined to a wheel chair after amputation.

P2. I sure have! Have a chair.

C3. No, thanks, been sitting all day.

Why not accept this little gesture of hospitality. You turn attention to your activity so he continues talking about you.

P3. Been keeping you busy this week?

C4. Don't let them keep me too busy — how about you?

Good, you show interest in him; turn it from yourself.

P4. Been pretty slow with me. This (showing me his foot) keeps the nurses busy though.

C5. It does?

In this case it is good to be brief, so he can elaborate if he wishes.

P5. Yeah. (Laughs.) They gotta be in here most of the time bathing it, etc.

Humor as safety valve for tension.

C6. Well, that's what they're here for.

(Pause.)

P6. My boy was just here to see me.

C7. He was?

P7. Yeah, he and his wife drove over. Like to have you meet him.

C8. I believe I saw him leaving your room.

P8. Yeah, that was him. Drove over here from Next City.

(Slight pause.)

P9. Fine boy. He's going to go places.

C9. Was that his first visit?

Are you trying to find out if the boy has neglected his father these past three weeks? If so, it's a bit too direct.

P10. Yeah, his job keeps him pretty busy, you know, salesman.

Notice how father defends him.

(Pause.)

C10. Is your heel better? It doesn't look as brown as it did last week.

Are you anxious to get into what you believe to be his big problem tonight? He'll mention it if he wants to discuss it.

P11. No, it isn't as brown. They scraped it last week.

C11. Say, how did things go last Saturday?

Remember it is you who changed the topic from his son to his heel. Perhaps he is not ready to talk about it yet. Why hurry?

P12. Pretty good. It's wonderful what they can do with operations nowadays.

His statement is ambivalent if he said, "*Pretty* good," which means not too good; but on the other hand, "they can do wonderful things" — but will they for him?

C12. They can do some marvelous things.

P13. All they did was scrape the sore. Tried to get it to drain.

C13. They thought scraping would do it?

Good — you respond with about the same tone of uncertainty that he expressed.

P14. Yeah.

(Rather long pause.)

I guess they didn't have much luck.

C14. They didn't?

Again you do well to be brief. Let him elaborate if he wishes.

P15. No. They're going to amputate tomorrow.

(I'm not sure what look came over my face. It's what I had been waiting for. And I thought I knew how I'd react. I guess it was his matter-of-fact way of putting it that threw me for a loss.)

This is the kind of situation in which it pays to have trained yourself in objectivity. It is most helpful if at such times you can actually be calm and not appear shocked. But, remember, it's hard not to appear shocked if you actually are.

C15. Amputate?

P16. Yeah, I'm scheduled for surgery tomorrow.

Your response in C15 is sufficient.

(Long pause.)

I'm glad you waited and didn't rush in with a lot of comment.

P17. Can't figure it out.

C16. Can't figure what out?

P18. Why . . .

(Pause.)

Why should I be asked to lose my leg?

C17. It's awfully hard to understand and even harder to take.

Excellent response because you are indicating that you understand his feelings, his real problem.

(Pause again. When P. did be-
gin to talk, however, the words came rapidly.)

P19. Ya know — I've led what I'd call a damn clean life. Pardon the French, but I've worked hard, kept my family well — been a good father and husband. I have my own code to live by, and it's a Christian code. I'm not greedy; I'd give my shirt off my back to my neighbor if he needed it. . . . But I've never really been much on this religion.

Theologically, this man believes in a God of direct and proportional retribution.

Underlying guilt feelings being gingerly expressed, almost rising to the surface.

(The first time in three calls that the word "religion" or anything connected with it has been mentioned.)

Now that he does bring it up, what will you do with it?

C18. You've never belonged to church?

Isn't this a rather superficial re-
sponse? He could have said all he did in P19 and still be a nominal church member, as many churches count membership.

P20. No, I haven't. (A possible hint of remorse in his tone.)

Is this God's way of showing me my mistake?

Here is an invitation to preach a sermonette, which may satisfy your needs; but the real problem is how to help him to find a suitable and adequate answer to his searching.

C19. I don't think God acts in that way. After all, there are pretty wicked men on this earth that lead an awfully happy life.

P21. That's just it. I've led a pretty happy life. Could never see any need for going to church — I was content doing pretty good for myself. But now . . .

(Slight pause.)

I don't know. I don't see where I've deserved this.

C20. It's hard to understand.

(Pause.)

But you know — leading a good life or a bad life doesn't necessarily determine how we're treated by God on earth. There have been some pretty good churchgoing people that have suffered all kinds of hardships.

(I here related very briefly the story of Job.)

P22. Well, I've endured some pretty rough living in my time — guess I'll get through this too.

C21. We have to take things as they come, don't we?

P23. Yeah.

(Slight pause.)

This is strange comfort, besides being an impersonal generalization. Rather say, " You wonder if God is punishing you for not having been much on religion? "

Notice how ambivalent his statement is: " I've led a good life . . . but," and, " I don't know." Show him that you understand his confusion and uncertainty and searching.

So far so good.

Your approach here is much the same as in C19. You give him the answer backed up by an illustration to clinch the point. Are you sure he's ready yet for the answer. He hasn't gotten enough off his chest yet to be able to accept an intellectual answer. All he's done so far is make a few tentative admissions of fault; but most of his time has been spent building up his defenses of his somewhat " good life."

See, he would be willing to tell what's really on his heart and mind if you'll give him a chance.

Rhetorical questions are not very helpful because they preclude all but one answer. You are also precluding much further discussion by this conclusive remark.

He feels that since you have given a conclusive and terminal statement, there's not much use pursu-

How much longer you got in school?

ing it further. Therefore, he shifts the topic of conversation away from his real problem and socializes.

C22. Another semester.

P24. Guess you'll be glad to get out.

C23. Uh-huh. Listen, I'd better go now. Get a good night's rest. And I'll see you next Friday.

Do you think this person was ready for a prayer to help him face the crisis of amputation and to bring before God his vague questionings? I feel he would have been receptive to such an opportunity since it was he who first brought up the religious questions.

P25. Do that. 'By.

V. *Evaluation*

1. *Summary and analysis:* After small talk of the week's activities, his son's visit, etc., I put to P. the direct question about the condition of his heel (knowing all along what was in store for him). His reply gave no hint about his condition. It took another direct question to get the truth out. Finally, he told me about the amputation and went into reasons for it. His situation, then, is considerably worse than last week.

Patients generally do not discuss a painful subject until they are ready and willing, no matter how we probe or pull.

His situation is about the same, only now he has been confronted by the reality.

Just as shocking as the news of the amputation was the spiritual significance of this visit. It's the first time anything connected with religion has been mentioned; but when it came, we really got into it.

You did not let him get into it nearly so much as he was willing to.

2. *Self-criticism:* I tend to bring up small talk. I don't know why

I made the remark about his son's visit in C9. It may have raised the question in his mind, "Why hasn't he been over before?"

Glad you're aware of the various meanings and implications for the patient here.

The critical part of the call was a complete failure. As I look back on this call, I can see that I tried to force him to talk about what *I* thought was his problem. Then when he mentioned it, I shut him off. I can see where I seized upon P19 as an opportunity to expound at length and left him and his questions far behind. It made me feel good to give him this speech. I could sense that I was losing him during C20. After that he was obviously through talking about his problem. That's why I took my departure at that time. I had fully intended to offer prayer for him, but after he shut me off at P22, I lost my opportunity and courage.

Not "complete" because he did make a beginning and verbalize some of his doubts and concerns. You may be able to help him continue this in another call.

You show some good understanding of your own motivations here.

Sorry to have to remind you that you shut him off at C21. You could still have offered prayer, including the many needs he has expressed.

This has been a most beneficial call for me; although I'm afraid the insights I've gained into pastoral care were at the expense of P.

There was no other person providing pastoral care; and if you had not seen him, he would have had none at all. Remember his comment at end of last call, "It's good to know someone's thinking of you."

3. *Opportunities:* Naturally I want to see this man next time and try to help him to accept and adjust to his amputation and what it will mean for his future life.

Do not be too discouraged in your progress. You are becoming aware of many of your mistakes and have the honest desire to improve, which is vital and good.

4. *Time:* Twelve to fifteen minutes. It seemed about right, except that I realize I left rather abruptly.

Series B. Continued

RECORD OF PASTORAL CALL

Student _____ *Seminarian Jones*

Course _____ *Pastoral Counseling, Sem.*

Supervisor _____ *Professor Belgum*

Code No. _____ I, 4, C.H.

Date of Call _____ *March 19, 195–*

Type _____ *Surgical*

I. *Preliminary Information*

Originally this call was assigned by the supervisor, but I have come to look forward to these calls because a fairly good rapport has been established between P. and myself.

Yes, your attitude has changed from casual interest to a genuine pastoral concern.

The reason for P.'s hospitalization is gangrene in his left heel. He is extremely conscientious about his work, as maintenance foreman on the railroad. He has been in the hospital over four weeks, and had no idea originally that his infection would take such a long period for treatment.

A disappointing surprise to quite a few patients.

At the last call it was learned that P. was scheduled to have his foot or leg amputated. This was shocking to me and I'm quite sure to P. also. He was greatly puzzled by why he should be asked to part with a leg, putting the blame partly on the fact that he didn't belong to church and this was his punishment for it. It could be for no other reason since he had led such a " good life."

II. *Preparation*

There were several things I wished to accomplish in this call. I wanted to continue our conversation at the point where I lost him last time — the reason for his operation. I was interested in knowing how much of his leg had to be amputated and how disabling it would be for him. Also I was concerned about his reaction to the operation of last Saturday.

Could be useful, but I hope you'll let *his* interests guide you primarily.

Guard against any feelings about his amputation that might be classified as morbid curiosity.

I meditated as I went down the hall, asking God's help that I might not fumble and blunder as I had at the previous call. I was extremely concerned about the man's understanding of the cause of his loss of leg. At the same time, I realized that it was impossible for him to look at it objectively; so I decided that arguing or even intellectual conversation dealing with such matters was entirely out.

Such an attitude will be a big help. We should always ask God to go with us on such important business.

Helpful insight. You are planning on meeting the man on his own level. Starting where he is, and working from there.

I was prepared to see a man, who had two legs last week, sitting or lying crippled by the loss of one leg. I realized this could be quite a shock to me even though I had tried to prepare myself for it. It was a good thing I had prepared myself for the worst because most of it was gone.

Continued work with the sick of all conditions should help you get over being shocked at unpleasant sights and smells.

III. *Observations*

As I entered the room, P. was sitting on the far side near the window. He was in a collapsible wheel chair. His left leg had been taken off just above the knee. He was doing nothing but sitting and, it seemed, staring. There were quite a few flowers on the dresser top. The cards were stacked on the dresser in a neat pile. The bed was neatly made, which indicated that he had not spent much time in it lately.

I gather he was alone in the room since you mention no other patient or visitor.

IV. *Interpersonal Relationship*

C1. Hello, Mr. P., how are you today?

A friendly opener.

P1. Pretty fair. How are you? (Smiling.)

C2. No complaints. You been pretty fair?

You turn it back to him, which is good; try to reflect his mood or feeling tone.

P2. Yeah, they took 'er off Saturday. Pointing to left thigh. It gets pretty tender here at the stub. Guess it's from being drawn back when I sit. But even at that I'm more comfortable than in bed.

C3. It was removed at the knee.

You respond more to the fact than how he feels about it.

P3. Yeah, right above the knee joint. The doctor said that they could have taken it off little by little, but I'd end up losing this much anyway — so I might as well lose it all at once.

C4. The gangrene would spread that much?

More important, has P. accepted the fact the doctors needed to remove so much?

P4. It had gotten into the blood stream, so it would have been just a matter of time. Guess I'm lucky to be alive.

C5. It can be pretty treacherous stuff.

Rather respond to his feeling of this having been a crisis.

P5. This gadget (pointing to wheel chair) sure comes in handy. I had been using one of the hospital chairs, but they practically killed me getting in and out.

C6. They have a deeper seat, don't they?

P6. They sure do. When I saw my wife bringing this one in I couldn't figure out what it was. It was all collapsed. But I'm sure glad. She rented it, but if we decide to keep it, all we paid in rent will go toward the purchase price.

C7. Is that right? Then the money in rent won't be wasted.

His wife's part in this rehabilitation might even be more significant than the money — refer to her.

P7. Nope, and it's a darn handy thing to have around.

(Pause.)

I've seen a lot of men around without their legs. See a lot of them in the yards. You'd never guess that they were wearing an artificial leg.

(P. related stories about men he had known: a young fellow with an artificial leg who had joined the circus; the men he knew who worked around the railroad yards who had slipped under the engines, etc., and lost legs.)

Now he is saying in his own words what you tried to say for him last time when you said, "We have to take things as they come, don't we?" Only this time he's ready for this next step of accepting reality.

So I guess it's something you can get used to.

(Wife enters room at this point.)

Wife. Hello, you're Mr. J., aren't you?

C8. Yes.

Wife. We were talking about you yesterday, thinking how nice it's been having you drop in to see Mr. P. like this.

C9. He was just telling me about your surprise.

This is good. You acknowledge Mrs. P. and her contribution, but refocus attention on P.

(I turned my head back to Mr. P. so that he could continue.)

P8. Oh, I'll get lots of good out of this.

(Pause.)

It scared me something awful when they first told me I was to lose my leg. I didn't want to think of myself as a cripple. When they told me last Friday, I laid there and cried.

He had had more feelings about this than you had guessed last Friday.

C10. I can certainly understand why you would.

You show a helpful acceptance of his feelings. Big, strong men often feel it is unacceptable for them to express their true emotions, especially tears.

P9. But after stopping to think about all the people I knew with artificial limbs, it made me feel better. We have a cottage up on the lake. It's a winter place, so I'll just retire and move up there for about five or six months.

C11. For five or six months?

If you don't understand something it's quite all right to ask for clarification.

P10. Yeah, it'll take that long before they can fit me for an artificial leg. There'll be some shrinkage, etc.

C12. I see.

P11. We have an awfully nice cottage. (He gave the details of all there'd be for him to do there.)

Wife. There'll be plenty to keep him busy. He's feeling much better about the whole thing now than he was. I always said that when the Lord takes something away, he always gives something in return.

P12. The only thing that bothers me is these four walls. I've been in here a long time looking at 'em, and it gets tiresome.

C13. They kind of get you down after a while.

This shows him that you can appreciate what he feels about his situation.

P13. They sure can. I've never been in prison, not even in jail; but I know now what it's like and I sure never want to go.

Wife. Oh, it can be lots worse than this.

Typical lack of empathy, but with the good intention of cheering up the patient. We avoid it.

P14. But I should be out before the week's up. Then I'll have plenty of space around me. I'll be more contented with lots of room around me.

C14. You think you'll be more content at the cottage.

A responsive statement.

P15. Yeah, until I get my leg. I'll get along O.K. I believe in prayer. Even though I don't belong to church or anything, I do have faith in prayer, and a lot of people have said they are praying for me. I know it'll do some good.

C15. I'd like to offer a prayer before I leave.

A naturally fitting time and place in view of both his and his wife's recent comments.

P16. You have to go now?

C16. I'd better.

P17. O.K.

C17. (I gave a prayer here concerning thankfulness for a Father who is vitally interested and concerned with us, even the sparrows, thankfulness that he's constantly so close to us, knowing and feeling our needs, and fulfilling those needs as he sees fit to our good.)

Why not quote this prayer verbatim as you do the other conversation?

It seems that the tone of this prayer is quite appropriate. We want this to be the patient's prayer as well as ours.

P18. Thanks so much. Now you be sure to drop in and see me if you're ever near the lake. (Detailed directions followed on how to find his cottage.)

This hospitality is a kind of note of appreciation.

C18. I just may do that sometime.

P19. Don't forget it. I've surely enjoyed your visits here.

C19. I've enjoyed talking with you.

P20. It's good to know someone's interested in you.

C20. You take care of yourself.

A bit too trite. A simple "Goodby" does just as well.

P21. I will. 'By.

V. *Evaluation*

1. *Summary and analysis:* All that I had wanted to accomplish in this call was done, except the vital point of why his leg had to come off and was it punishment from God. This might have come up if his wife had not come to visit. I found out that he had a brighter view of the situation now that he had had a little time to think things over and accept his new situation.

P. had identified himself with others in the same predicament. He saw they were apparently getting along all right, and consequently he would too. Undoubtedly the mood of depression in the previous call reflected the fact that he had been stunned by the unexpected news of an impending amputation.

Remember how you tried to get him to identify with Job?

He had me completely fooled as to his age. I discovered that he is sixty years old! — and not forty as I had thought. Therefore, he is only five years from retirement anyway. I presume he can then draw his pension, or perhaps even now. I am unaware how much of a

You were wise not to pry into this matter since he did not choose to bring it up.

financial strain this total change of plans will be for him. He did not discuss it.

2. *Self-criticism:* Actually, I feel that I have really grown in my own appreciation of crisis and tragedy through ministering to Mr. P. I also recognize a great need for further emotional maturation on my part in order to be able to cope with such events and situations, which will undoubtedly befall many of my parishioners through the years. I still need to work on my weakness of seeking information and facts per se. What these mean to the patient is far more important than the facts and events themselves. From Mr. P. I have learned that one must always be prepared to meet the unexpected without shock or surprise, especially in ministering to the sick.

3. *Opportunities:* Although I will not see P. again, I know there are many problems ahead for him in his readjustment of a spiritual, emotional, and financial nature. His activity will be limited as well as his income. I believe he could be led by a patient pastor to desire the fellowship of the church.

4. *Time of this call:* Nine or ten minutes.

Not only have you grown through this relationship; I believe you rendered a real service to Mr. P. If we have a real loving concern for people, God can use us in ministering to people in need in spite of our occasional blunderings.

He will have to be a nonjudgmental pastor who is willing to meet this man where he is, and work from there.

CONCLUSION: THE LARGER PERSPECTIVE

WHEN a pastor or student of clinical pastoral training becomes excited about the dynamic possibilities of pastoral care, he needs to guard against the narrow-mindedness of specialization by bearing in mind the larger perspective of his total ministry and the whole field of theological education. It is unfortunate that to some the prospect of a parish ministry seems dull when contrasted with the prestige and excitement of a great city hospital or the fascination of working with the mysterious forces of mental illness.

Such devotees are tempted to depreciate the parish ministry as a routine of budget-raising and superficial handshaking and prefer a "chance to do just pastoral counseling." One student said, "I can't stand ladies' aids, church council meetings, and the like; I want to serve people who are in real need." The fact is that an alert pastor, who is available and recognizes golden opportunities, will find even in a small parish that he is confronted by numerous people in dire need of pastoral care, perhaps a larger number than many a professional counselor or social worker would consider a maximum "case load." How, then, does the clinical pastoral education described in this book fit into the larger pattern of theological education?

CLINICAL TRAINING AS ONE PART OF PASTORAL THEOLOGY

It should be borne in mind that there are many skills and services required of a pastor besides individual pastoral care and counseling. He must not neglect his preaching responsibility, but constantly try to improve it in style and content. He must improve his understanding of the principles and techniques of good church administration, in regard to personnel (paid and volunteer) and program as well as property. Just as counseling has its function of restoring spiritual and mental health, wholesome Christian education plays a vital part in the prevention of such breakdowns requiring therapy. So, also, the fields of evangelism, church music, and worship offer great challenges to the pastor who has not closed his mind to these opportunities by giving his attention exclusively to any one phase of practical theology.

To broaden the perspective of the theological picture, mention should be made of the other three traditional divisions of theological study, namely: historical, systematic, and exegetical theology.

Historical theology cites many fads in the experience of the Church and its ministry. The Oxford Movement flourished on the overemphasis of a useful function. During the twenties, the extremely popular religious education movement put thousands of church gymnasiums into temporary use until other emphases came to the fore. Likewise, the " Akron Plan " of church building had its day. There is, therefore, a need to evaluate the clinical training program not only in terms of the rest of the Church's program, but also to see it in its historical perspective, in order that its useful benefits may continue longer than the average fad.

Systematic theology is another integral part of the seminarian's training that can never be minimized or sacrificed while the student is becoming zealous in the area of pastoral care. The student and the pastor both need a broad theoretical and philosophical framework or foundation for all their pastoral work, a system of thought and belief that will unify their whole ministry. The student needs to integrate his findings in the human laboratory of suffering and experience with the teachings and doctrines of the Church. It is not even good mental hygiene to believe one thing in theory but act differently in practice.

Sound exegesis and good Biblical scholarship help the pastor see the prophetic as well as the pastoral side of the ministry, the methods of pastoral care used in the Scripture, and the limitations of counseling in cases of extreme social injustice (cf. Amos) or hypocrisy (e.g., Christ's cleansing the Temple). The Bible cannot be used effectively in pastoral care if it is not well known and clearly understood by the pastor. So we see that pastoral counseling and "good relationship" are not a substitute for sound theological scholarship and competence in this as in any other department. The good pastor will continue to be the one who has the well-rounded theological education and the larger perspective.

PERSONAL AND PROFESSIONAL GROWTH

"A little learning is a dangerous thing" is a precautionary proverb that is especially applicable to the field of pastoral counseling. A theological student or pastor who has completed an introductory semester or summer course in this field should certainly not even suggest that he is equipped to give therapy to all comers. Rather, it is hoped that an introductory survey and a little clinical experience will demonstrate to him his limitations as well as his resources and potentialities. The quickest way for the pastor to lose the respect and co-operation of other members of the health team (surgeons, psychiatrists, social workers, psychologists, etc.) is for him to assume a professional competence beyond his real capacity, training, and ability. Such arrogance is hardly appropriate for a Christian pastor.

The pastor who assumes that, because he has read some articles and a book on psychosomatic medicine, he can distinguish between functional and organic illness may well find himself trying to counsel a parishioner out of a brain tumor. Likewise, a pastor needs to recognize his limitations in dealing with persons having severe, prolonged depression, delusions, hallucinations, marked and sudden personality change, feelings of persecution, etc. Even a skilled physician with intensive psychiatric training and experience and the resources of a mental hospital will find such problems an involved and difficult challenge. Therefore, the clergyman exhibits personal and professional growth to the degree in which he is able to recognize his limitations and make constructive referral to the professional services of other therapists and practitioners.

Personal growth toward a mature personality adjustment is essential. A pastor cannot help others with their problems if he is too involved with his own inner conflicts and emotional maladjustments. He needs to have relatively good mental hygiene and be relatively free from crippling neuroses; and if he should need help (including psychotherapy), he should not be too proud to admit it and take steps to secure such. One pastor, who had carried around a painful neurosis for over a decade, balked at the expense of one interview a week for a prolonged series of psychotherapy; but he no doubt would gladly have paid more than that to save his left leg from amputation. In dollars and cents he put more value on his left leg and its use than upon his mental health and release from this crippling panic.

Neurotic self-concern and egocentricity, lack of self-confidence, and unrealistic goals interfere with the establishment of spontaneous and creative relationships with parishioners as well as minimize the degree of rapport so essential to effective pastoral counseling. The minister with an emotional need to dominate other people or manipulate them for his own purposes is not likely to find parishioners bringing their problems to him. (Some won't even tell their pastor they're going to the hospital, for fear he'll browbeat them when they're flat on their back!) Such a man needs personal growth, a change of basic attitudes, or emotional re-education. It is not enough to have sound doctrine and theory; the pastor must have the personality that will allow him to act in accordance with his Christian faith. He should be the first to admit the need for growth in grace and truth and self-understanding. It is even said of our blessed Lord that he "increased in wisdom and in stature, and in favor with God and man " (Luke 2:52).

THE VITAL SENSE OF VOCATION

Although there may be times when calling on the sick seems dull and routine and tiresome, the pastor must keep alive within his soul an awareness of the greatness of his calling, the eternal significance of the gospel ministry, and the incalculable value of the individual person in the sight of God. The same God who created life is continually and vitally concerned about the progress, welfare, and destiny of that soul. We call on the sick because we have a mandate of love to do so in the words of Christ: I was sick and you visited me. . . . Truly, I say to you, as you did it to one of the least of these my brethren, you did it to me " (Matt. 25:36, 40).

Unless the pastor has experienced the grace, comfort, and guidance of God in his own life's struggle, he will hardly be able to pass
on these blessings to others in need. The spirit of Paul, as he writes
to the church in Corinth, is a glorious example of the true pastor,
who does not trust in his own power but lets God work through
him:

" Blessed be the God and Father of our Lord Jesus Christ, the
Father of mercies and God of all comfort, who comforts us in all
our affliction, so that we may be able to comfort those who are in
any affliction, with the comfort with which we ourselves are comforted by God " (II Cor. 1:3, 4).

SUGGESTED READINGS

SUGGESTED READINGS

Allport, Gordon W., *The Individual and His Religion*. The Macmillan Company, 1950.

Bergsten, Gote, *Pastoral Psychology*. The Macmillan Company, 1951.

Cabot, R. D., and Dicks, Russell L., *The Art of Ministering to the Sick*. The Macmillan Company, 1936.

Dicks, Russell L., *Pastoral Work and Personal Counseling* (rev. ed.). The Macmillan Company, 1949.

Dunbar, Helen Flanders, *Emotions and Bodily Changes* (3d ed.). Columbia University Press, 1946.

Fletcher, Joseph, *Morals and Medicine*. Princeton University Press, 1954.

Hiltner, Seward, *Pastoral Counseling*. Abingdon Press, 1949. *Clinical Pastoral Training*. Commission on Religion and Health, Federal Council of the Churches of Christ in America, 1945.

Hulme, William E., *How to Start Counseling*. Abingdon Press, 1955.

Johnson, Paul E., *Psychology of Pastoral Care*. Abingdon Press, 1953.

McNeill, John T., *A History of the Cure of Souls*. Harper & Brothers, 1951.

Maves, Paul B., and Cedarleaf, J. Lennart, *Older People and the Church*. Abingdon Press, 1949.

Oates, Wayne, *The Bible in Pastoral Care*. The Westminster Press, 1951.

Roberts, David E., *Psychotherapy and a Christian View of Man*. Charles Scribner's Sons, 1950.

Rogers, Carl R., *Client-centered Therapy*. Houghton Mifflin Co., 1951.

Veterans Administration, *The Chaplain's Manual:* Veterans Administration Manual, M6–3, Revised, Washington 25, D.C., 1953.

Weatherhead, Leslie D., *Psychology, Religion and Healing.* Abingdon Press, 1951.

Wise, Carroll A., *Pastoral Counseling: Its Theory and Practice.* Harper & Brothers, 1951.

Wood, Leland F., *Pastoral Counseling in Family Relationships.* Federal Council of Churches, 1948.

Young, Richard K., *The Pastor's Hospital Ministry.* Broadman Press, 1954.